The Life Recovery Method:

Autism treatment from a trauma perspective

By

Robert Cox, MA, LPC, NCC

Editing assistance: Emily Crawford-Margison

Printed by CreateSpace
Available from Amazon.com and other retail outlets

ISBN-13:
978-1539789017

ISBN-10:
1539789012

"The first time I sat down next to Robert during a clinical staffing meeting I thought who in the world is this man? He didn't look up, just kept working on his iPad. About 10 minutes in he looked up, took advantage of a lull in the conversation and proceeded to educate all of us on this child that he had only met once. Robert has a unique ability to assess behavior and environments in a matter of seconds or minutes. And to then provide a list of real treatment ideas that are simple and highly effective. I have worked with Robert on my most difficult cases and been consistently impressed by the simplicity of his ideas and amazed by his incredible knowledge. Robert is a fierce advocate and has walked along side many families to help them find hope and progress in very challenging situations. I am thankful to have had the opportunity to learn from and work with such a gifted clinician and scholar. I look forward to the inspiration he will share throughout this book. Parents and professionals alike will leave this book with hope, purpose and confidence." --
Lori Wheelhouse, MA, LCPC, Clinical Director, KVC Prairie Ridge Children's Hospital

One third of the individuals served by Special Needs Services of Ray County have a diagnosis of autism. Many of those individuals have experienced a trauma that reemerges in episodes of self-harm, depression, harm to others, and isolation. Mr. Cox has taught Mindfulness Training to individuals with autism that has allowed these individuals to move their thoughts past the trauma. I credit Mr. Cox with encouraging individuals to focus on what their life can become. Individuals are now making eye contact with others and speaking for themselves. They are working alongside their neighbors in competitive jobs. Many have left their natural homes and are learning how to live with supports in their community. Without the assessment and on-going therapy provided by Mr. Cox, our agency would still be responding to 911 calls and attempting to console desperate caregivers. – **Suzan Breen, Executive Director, Special Needs Services of Ray County**

"Robert is the first provider to focus on my son's sensory needs as a primary treatment. Since we have implemented a sensory based therapeutic ideal, my son has made the most progress he has in years! He is no longer regressing, but PRO gressing. And more importantly, I got my sweet good natured, FUNNY kid back!" — **BL**

"After years of struggling with inappropriate and lack of social behaviors our son was diagnosed with Asperger's. During these same years and after diagnosis we went through several therapists with no success until 2015 when our son started working with Robert Cox and the use of mindfulness. The change in our son has been dramatic. Once very socially awkward, with no friends and behaviors that could have legal ramifications; he has made wonderful progress with the treatment he has been receiving." — **VA**

Contents

1. Acknowledgements   i
2. Introduction   iii
3. A Letter to Parents and Caregivers   viii
4. The Face of Autism   2
5. Trauma and the Brain   11
6. The Autistic Brain and Sensory Trauma   21
7. The Trauma Effects of Autism   28
8. Sensory Issues, Sensory Integration and   37
    Sensory Diets
9. The Use of Mindfulness Training   55
10. Autism in the Schools   73
11. Social Development, Autism and Trauma   86
12. Employment Issues   99
13. Treatment Methods, Issues and Direction   109
14. Final Notes to Parents   119
15. Appendix A: Sensory Assessment   129
16. Works Cited   134

Acknowledgements

I have had the real pleasure and luck to have been able to work with some profoundly talented people in this field. Among them was my friend, Beth Sherrell, who pushed me and pushed me to write a book. Who kept saying that a solid resource was needed for parents, educators and professionals alike. Who showed faith in me even when my faith failed in myself and who checked an overblown sense of ego (as only true friends will) when it got too big. Without her pushing and seeing in me what I could not see in myself at times, this probably would not have been finished (late or otherwise).

Lori Wheelhouse, who accused me of having a mind like a steel trap in a meeting after we had first met and who has since seen me as a colleague (which is a huge deal when she is so profoundly amazing as a practitioner herself) and, I hope, as a constant friend. Again, she provided a cheering voice that helped lift me out of the land of self-criticism that we get trapped in at times.

Suzan Breen, who constantly has touted me as the miracle worker in her county (deserved or not) and whose vision of better treatment and fuller inclusion has so infected me that it drives me forward into my own vision of creating a trauma treatment center in rural MO that I believe can become a shining example of what treatment can look like in rural communities and how inclusion can benefit all.

To Beth Russell, who is a rock star trauma therapist and had the grace to call me "colleague" early on. She is responsible for rocking my intellectual world and really changing the direction of my practice very early on.

To all of the amazing service coordinators, therapists, school administrators and counselors who have helped me along the way by simply being an inspirational example of work ethic and hope never-ending.

Certainly not least, to my family. My wife Stancia, who has propped me up by sharing her belief in me even when I couldn't see it, and my two amazing children, Tristn and Kerrie Ann, who have been my driving inspiration every moment of the last 13 years. You are my heart and my reason for being and what grounds me when the work becomes overwhelming.

Without these people in my life, this book would not be before you. Without them, I would not be who or where I am.

Introduction

I have been working with individuals on the spectrum for more than 20 years now. I began in about 1993 as a direct care provider. Essentially my job was to go to the home and assist individuals with learning new skills, working on behavioral objectives, and other goals set out by the team which involved the parents, the individual and a state-assigned case manager with the division of developmental disabilities. Specific learning goals would be decided upon and broken into teaching steps, and my job was to assist the individual under the direction of a psychologist or therapist with meeting those goals.

From the beginning, I saw something wrong with the system as it existed. For example, many individuals with autism exhibit "stimming" behaviors. The flapping of hands is one that is very prominent. These behaviors were, at that time, thought to be undesirable and the goal was often to stop the stimming because it interfered with social development by setting them apart. In one instance, I was supposed to direct the young man to sit on his hands when this occurred. I never did. Even then, I felt this young man was using the behavior to keep himself calm and it seemed cruel to take that away. It has always seemed to me that in a compassionate society, we would make room for behaviors that people use to soothe themselves. That we would at least insist a little less that they fit into our predetermined box of normalcy.

Over the next 14 years, I would be content to do direct care. Without bragging, I can say I was very good at it. In my own recovery, I had learned to use mindfulness to calm myself in stressful situations by regulating my breathing. This had the effect of de-escalating situations even after they had become explosive, so I was the crisis team for many of my employers, called into homes when the meltdowns were out of control. Over those 14 years, I only had to physically restrain a client for his/her protection twice, and both of those times, I believed I had failed in some capacity. But what I noticed were some very similar responses to sensory issues and situations that confused both caregivers and individuals who were trying to cope.

Over the next two and a half years, I took a full-time job as a service coordinator contracted to the division of developmental disabilities in Missouri. I also began an accelerated Master's degree program in counseling where my focus was trauma and addictions. I noticed similarities among the trauma responses I was seeing in clients, what I was discovering in research and what I had observed in autism. In the research, I found nothing really relating the two, though I did hear it being spoken about by trauma therapists like Bessel Van der Kolk in his foundational work *The Body Keeps the Score* and by other neuroscientists in their works.

I attended workshops on assessing sensory needs and creating sensory diets. I found in the research that when sensory diets were implemented in effective ways, the need for behavioral services went down and behaviors declined. I wondered why, if high-functioning individuals showed the same cognitive abilities as the neurotypical population, mindfulness and cognitive therapy wouldn't work better for them than the currently used ABA therapies. The consistent answer I got was that ABA is an "evidence-based" approach, which generally was meant to shut down discussion and keep the flow of therapy dollars headed in that direction.

At the time, I had no dog in that fight. I was not a therapist. I was, however, noticing methods in research that worked for clients with trauma. Trauma responses and reactions that looked a lot like behavioral responses I was seeing in autism. Similar symptoms like anxiety, OCD and depression in the neurotypical population were being well controlled with these methods and I began to see that they could be used with autism. These were methods that could become "evidence-based" if we began doing the work and gathering the evidence. So, I continued digging.

By the time I graduated with my master's, I had created my own private practice in Liberty, MO. I have been treating individuals there, lecturing on these methods and getting powerful results. So powerful, in fact, that I was recruited by an outfit in Richmond, MO (Special Needs Services of Ray County) and was provided with an office there to begin seeing clients. I've expanded to the point that I have now opened a trauma treatment center in that town and currently have another therapist contracting with me following these methods. I have included a few testimonials in this book from parents and professionals in the field who have seen the results. This book is an attempt to get the theory and the methods out there. It is, as my lectures over the past several years have been, an attempt to change the way we see and think about the treatment and expression of autism.

I sincerely hope you find it useful in your journey whether you are a teacher, therapist, case manager, caregiver or parent.

A Letter to Parents and Caregivers

I wanted to take some space here to speak to caregivers and parents. I want to encourage you to read through this book even if, at times, it feels like you are lost in a mess of psycho-neuro-babble. I want you to continue through because at the end, I am going to include a chapter for you that will, with luck, wrap up what we have talked about in a way that will help you to start implementing supports for the individuals in your lives today. So much of what I have seen over the past 22+ years is parents and caregivers feeling alone in the wilderness. Parents who cannot find services for their children. There is nothing worse than feeling like there is help, but that you are ill-equipped to find it, while your child is suffering.

Professionals are often of less help than they could or should be, as well. I have been told repeatedly by parents that they were blamed for systems that "should" be working because they are evidence-based, and told that they are not implementing them properly.

In fact, I have had parents laugh and say it was refreshing that when they tell me they have tried something and it didn't work, I simply suggest something else. They were used to being told they weren't doing it right. I am here to tell you, that's not usually the case.

Autism is an extremely varied disorder in its expression. Even evidence-based approaches are not going to work for every child. This is not a perfect science. But if we start by listening to what those affected are telling us with both their voices and their behaviors, we can begin making it better. My system, at its heart, is based on that listening. Listening to why they don't feel safe and how they are coping with this themselves, even when the coping skills are inappropriate or limited in their effectiveness. We listen and use a few basic suggestions to make the world a safer place for them, and then implement some simple supports to begin moving forward.

What you are already doing is what you can do. You picked up this book because you already have the most important requirement for helping your child or loved one—the real desire to do so. Don't give up that desire, even when all roads seem closed. Even when governments, doctors and professionals are telling you there is nothing to be done, don't give up. Keep looking, keep pounding on doors. Rest when you need to without guilt and get back in the fight. Your loved one is counting on it.

While this book is written to try and change our views and treatment of autism and is, undoubtedly, going to be dense and aimed at professionals at times, I think you will find some important tools here, too. So, stick with me through the science-heavy parts and when we get to the end, I am hoping you will have found the hope and help you were looking for. If you still feel lost, reach out. I love to hear from those who are struggling because for me, it's an opportunity to do what I feel called to do.

Chapter 1: The Face of Autism

The term "autism" comes from the Greek root word "autos," meaning self, and has, since its beginning in the early 1900's, been used to describe many symptoms that create social distance and isolation, or a retreat into the self, in individuals. Early on, it was used to describe symptoms of schizophrenia and often referred to as "early childhood schizophrenia." In fact, we now know that schizophrenia and autism do have some shared genetic markers. Both disorders can result in disorganization of thinking and difficulties with communication, and can look a lot alike, even to professionals in the field. But there are fundamental differences that make them markedly different.

This view of autism as "self-turned-inward" has also created some myths that still persist today. Two among these that I will be discussing are the ideas that individuals with autism cannot navigate social spaces, and that individuals with autism do not feel empathy. Neither of these is necessarily true and both, as we will see, are often rooted in misconceptions that still persist about why someone with autism retreats. There is this fantasy out there that they are turning inward and ignoring the rest of the world because they have a richer inner world than the rest of us. While sometimes the internal experience is far better than the real world, it is not always the case. Often, the issue is that the noise created by trying to navigate the external world is so great that it sometimes becomes impossible to externalize through all of that. At other times, the retreat is purely about trying to feel safe in a world that is constantly assaultive. We will cover this and the idea that autistic individuals "don't get" social skills in later chapters.

In the DSM-V (Diagnostic and Statistical Manual of Psychiatric Disorders) the classification of autism has changed considerably. Prior to its implementation in 2015, autism disorders took on many names. The high-functioning end of the spectrum was "Asperger's," where individuals who were affected may not have been diagnosed until later in life when social deficits showed up. Then there was classic autism, where the sensory issues were more significant, communication problems may be present and social deficits were more significant. Along with these were Sensory Processing Disorder (SPD), Pervasive Developmental Disorder Not Otherwise Specified (PDD-NOS) and even Rhett's Syndrome. These disorders under the new DSM-V were put onto a continuum, or spectrum, of autism (although SPD is used as a separate diagnosis as we learn more about it). At the high-functioning end, we have what used to be known as Asperger's, or High Functioning Autism (HFA), and at the low end were the individuals with significant learning and social deficits driven by complex and extensive sensory issues.

With all the advances in science, we still do not know what "causes" autism. There simply is not any compelling evidence pointing to any cause. There is a lot of discussion about immunizations causing autism, but I have not yet seen any compelling evidence of this. In 1998, a British scientist, Dr. Andrew Wakefield, put forth a study linking immunizations to autism. In attempts to reproduce his research, scientists realized that not only was the data bad, but much of it had been faked. Dr. Wakefield was stripped of his medical license for faking the study by the British governing body, but the myth and the damage it caused in the world continues. Thousands of children go without important immunization, risking whole populations because of this falsified study. The popularity of conspiracy theories about big pharma and profiteering has helped to keep this theory going, but the fact remains that there simply is no credible evidence showing any link between the MMR vaccine and autism. In the most recent and largest study I could find of nearly 100,000 children, the finding was:

> *In this large sample of privately insured children with older siblings, receipt of the MMR vaccine was not associated with increased risk of ASD, regardless of whether older siblings had ASD. These findings indicate no harmful association between MMR vaccine receipt and ASD even among children already at higher risk for ASD. (Jain, et al. 2015)*

I am no fan of corporate medicine personally and, as someone who also specializes in addictions, I see the real damage that drug companies do in pushing their products. Conspiracy theories are both fun and entertaining and this is not the first time that vaccines have been blamed for this kind of thing. HIV was rumored to have been caused by the Polio vaccine and the claim was just as untrue. But my father grew up without the risk of polio because his was the first generation to test Jonas Salk's vaccine, and the disease has been unknown for the most part for more than half a century.

Is it possible that vaccines exacerbate already existing symptoms? I suppose it is, but I have yet to see any serious research outside of the documentary "Vaxxed," which was produced by the aforementioned and discredited Dr. Wakefield. Until there is solid research leading to something more, we are left with what to do about treatment, and there is much room for improvement in that area.

According to the data from Autism Speaks, autism is currently diagnosed in 1 of 68 children and boys are diagnosed more frequently than girls (4 to 1 ratio). In the past several years, the steep increase in numbers has leveled off and remained the same since

2014 (Autism Speaks, 2016). For the most part, this is because we are better at identifying and sorting out what is and is not autism. The recent push for earlier and earlier diagnosis may skew these numbers initially, but they will eventually level off.

Early on, autism was frequently confused with many disorders like Fragile-X, Angelman Syndrome and, as mentioned, schizophrenia. With the advent of genetic research, science has been able to sort out these disorders one from another. Often, however, it remains difficult for even professionals to differentiate between autism, ADHD, anxiety and other expressions early in the diagnosis. When they appear in conjunction with autism (comorbidity), it complicates the process of defining the primary diagnosis.

Much of the difficulty with early detection is that autism can resemble so many other issues, especially early in life. Is the child avoiding eye contact and bonding because he/she has autism or had he/she been ignored in the first year and is, thus, developing Reactive Attachment Disorder? Is the inability to attend to a task ADD or is it simply a sensory-seeking behavior due to autism? These disorders can look a lot like autism, especially early on, and confuse or confound early diagnosis. A team approach to diagnosis is often best for sorting out these issues. Often, we will see sensory issues where autism is concerned. Although sensory issues also develop with trauma, they are generally much different in expression and to the trained eye are different than the hypervigilance produced by trauma. I have frequently been called by case workers who felt a child had autism only to find out they were pulled from a violent home and had clients from violent homes where there were underlying sensory issues not otherwise explained that would indicate autism. It can become quickly complicated and entangled and is further evidence that autism and trauma affect the brain in some very similar ways.

In a discussion with my colleague, Beth, one afternoon, I was complaining about the push for earlier and earlier diagnosis and how I felt the field was going to end up the way it did in earlier decades with ADHD when that disorder was seriously over-diagnosed. "What," I asked, "if it's not autism but ADD or Fragile-

X?" Her response was simple and valid. It doesn't matter what we call it early on, if we put supports in place to help account for the deficits in development and functioning and then find it's something else, we are simply ahead of the game. I think there is validity in this argument without regard to age or diagnosis. We are dealing with what we are dealing with, and calling it by a new name will not change that.

The disorder itself is amazingly varied and there is a saying among those coping with autism: *When you have met one person with autism, you have met one person with autism.* Some individuals will have severe sensory issues, leaving them in a world of confusion, anxiety and severe learning deficits, while another will have almost no sensory issues but be left with extensive social deficits, such as the inability to take perspective when speaking to others. High-functioning individuals may well learn to control the sensory issues that do appear, but will still find relating to peers difficult, leading to socio-developmental delays.

Sensory issues can also be quite varied and, in many cases, change drastically with the onset of puberty and through developmental stages. We will delve deeply into sensory issues and the variety of types that can be expressed in later chapters, and I will include a checklist there for briefly assessing needs, although I recommend using the invaluable services of a good occupational and physical therapist (OT/PT) in making a complete and accurate assessment.

What it is important to know is that the disorder is widely varied from one individual to another, can mimic many other types of disorders and can change just when you think you've figured it out. This becomes an amazingly frustrating process for parents. In more than one instance, I have met with parents in tears because just when they have figured out their child's needs or seem to be making progress, everything changes, and they are, seemingly, back to square one. In one instance, I met with a mother whose child would only eat Michelena's frozen chicken nuggets because of sensory issues with food. She finally gave in and went to Sam's Club and got an entire freezer full of them. Not long after, his sensory sensitivities changed and then it was only hamburger patties that he would eat. As she related this story to me, she was in tears.

I have known other individuals who could not stand soft clothing and then, suddenly, would only wear flannel. Sensory issues often change around the time of puberty with the onslaught of hormonal upheaval. It is confusing and frustrating to the point of tears for parents at times.

This is the face of autism and what families deal with every day. In the coming chapters, we will be reviewing why sensory issues affect individuals the way they do and the research about autism and the brain, and begin looking at evidence-based methods for improving the lives of individuals struggling with autism.

Chapter 2: Trauma and the Brain

Before we delve into the autistic brain, I felt a cursory review of the emotional brain and how trauma can affect it would be appropriate. This is going to be only a general overview of how trauma works on the brain and how things like anxiety and PTSD begin to play out as a result of trauma events. For a fuller look at the brain and trauma, the works of Bessel van der Kolk, Peter Levine, Stephen Porges and Dan Siegel are ones I highly recommend.

Let's start by reviewing figure 2.1 which is a basic map of the emotional brain.

The thalamus is that large central feature and it is essentially responsible for gathering data from all of your senses. It is recording constantly what you see, hear, smell, feel and taste. It collects this information as a jumble of data that it then sends to your prefrontal cortex region and to the amygdala for processing. The prefrontal cortex is the area of your brain responsible for reasoning. Essentially it thinks through more complicated processes and decisions for you, weighing critical factors to help you decide on a course of action or reason through situations. In doing this, it uses the incoming sensory data from the thalamus.

Then we come to the amygdala. The amygdala is that small round nodule under the thalamus and its responsibility is to sort through the data sent by the thalamus and look for anything that might indicate danger. If it senses something in that data packet that could mean danger, it goes into action. It sets into motion the secretion of cortisol and adrenalin into the body and brain. This raises heart rate, makes respiration rapid and shallow, tightens the muscles and quickens the reflexes. Essentially, it triggers the fear response of the body and throws us into what is commonly known as fight, flight or freeze mode.

The amygdala makes this decision about safety and reacts in about 200 milliseconds. Whereas the frontal lobe will take about 3-5 seconds to sort through data and make a decision about action. If you are being pursued by a tiger, this is a crucial lapse in time, so, signaled by the amygdala, the brain goes into danger mode and it turns off the frontal and upper regions of the brain. Essentially, the amygdala creates a feedback loop where sensory information comes in through the body, is funneled to it through the thalamus and then sends signals to the body through the brainstem and the vagal nerve (which reaches from the lower brain all the way

14

into the organs of the lower body) without allowing
information to be moved into the upper parts of the brain
for processing first.

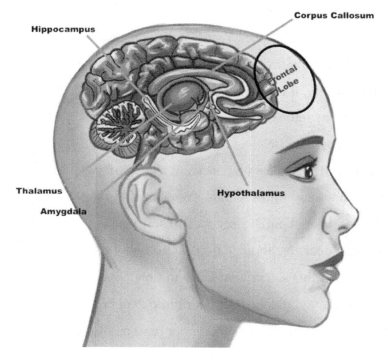

Figure 2.1

This is an executive function on the part of the brain. It
is doing its job and protecting the body from harm by

triggering the fight, flight or freeze response and taking
the decision-making part of the brain off line. In
addition, it triggers the secretion of cortisol and
adrenaline, which raise your heart rate, intensify your
senses, make your breathing rapid and shallow, tense
your muscles and create a state of heightened sensory
awareness. In other words, it prepares you for battle.

This is a fantastic system if there is a tiger behind
you. You need to quickly either pick up a stick or start
running, so you want the amygdala cutting down on
decision-making time. This is not such a great reaction
to have in the middle of Target while trying to shop. So
why would the fight-or-flight system trigger when I'm in
Target? This is where we begin with our discussion of
trauma and neural wiring for just a moment (stay with
me; I promise not to get too dense here).

Brain scientists and therapists have a saying: the
neurons that fire together wire together. For this
discussion, let's refer to figure 2.2, an image of neurons
(the black central cells in the image) and the connections
between them (the spindly fibers reaching from one to
the next). Notice in the first slide, representing a

newborn brain, there are only a few neurons and connections between them are sparse. The number of neurons as we age is constant unless there is damage to the brain, but the number of connections grows exponentially until we are about two years old, as you can see from the imagery. At age two, the connections begin to thin. This is when the neurons that are firing together begin to stay and the unused pathways begin to be pruned away. Just like a fruit tree farmer would prune his trees to produce larger, stronger fruit, the brain prunes away the unused neural connections to strengthen what remains.

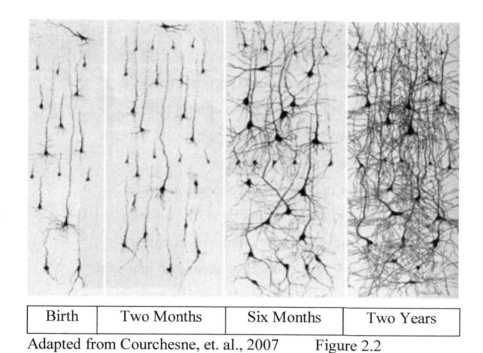

| Birth | Two Months | Six Months | Two Years |

Adapted from Courchesne, et. al., 2007   Figure 2.2

So, what exactly do we mean by firing together? My dog Viktor is very attuned to the sound of a Cheetos bag opening. He could recognize that sound from a mile away. It did not begin that way. It began with me sharing Cheetos with him, then he began to recognize that just before I handed him a Cheeto, I picked up an orange bag that crinkled, and then, a few seconds later, he was getting a Cheeto. Now, when he hears the bag, the neurons that register the sound of the bag in his brain also register the taste of the Cheetos and that food experience. He comes sprinting expectantly across the house with his mouth watering and a clumsy tail wagging. His neurons for the crinkling bag and the taste of the Cheeto have wired together.

In a similar but more negative way, a combat vet's brain may wire together the sound of explosions from weapons firing and horrible things happening around him and a 4th of July celebration and go into total meltdown mode over a few firecrackers. His brain has wired that sound of explosion with bad results, which he has seen happen directly after hearing that sound. The neurons for the sound and the result have wired together.

Anxiety results because even just seeing a firework can create the expectation of hearing the sound in the brain and trigger a post-traumatic reaction. This is what PTSD is all about. The trauma that individuals suffer can result in the stimulus (sights, sounds, smells) that were around when the trauma occurred triggering the brain's wiring and creating complete recall of the trauma.

In the case of PTSD, this trauma feels as if it is happening all over again and in the immediate moment. It is more than a memory. It is a re-experiencing of the trauma on a very real body level. So, let's look at how that happens and, because I promised not to get too dense in discussion here, I will keep it fairly elementary and simple.

Essentially, the hippocampus (see diagram 2.1 again) is the part of the brain that is responsible for storing new memories. In conjunction with the hypothalamus, it stores these in great detail so that when we recall, we can recall sensation and emotion associated with that memory intensely. It's how we are able to connect to a memory of our long-gone grandfather with just a picture. Suddenly, the memories of spending summer days with him come back to us and we feel some of those emotions intensely again. The hippocampus also transports the memory to the top of the brain and puts a time stamp on it so we remember it as a past event.

In the case of a trauma event, remember the top part of the brain is shut down because the amygdala and limbic response takes over. The hypothalamus hands off emotional memory to the hippocampus for storage, but it cannot store those memories because the top wing of the brain has been shut down by the amygdala, which is in protective mode. So, the memory never receives a time stamp and is sent to be stored deeper in the brain and in the tissues of the body as a sensory memory instead. Thus, the title of Bessel Van der Kolk's book, *The Body Keeps the Score*. Van der Kolk points out that the reintegration of the body and the brain through yoga and mindfulness techniques are among the best methods for treating trauma in conjunction with therapy (Van der Kolk, 2014). In fact, it is not uncommon for massage therapists and yoga teachers to have clients begin experiencing deep emotion they cannot find reason for when certain areas of the body are triggered. Indeed, in my own practice with mindfulness and with clients I teach, this experience is shared. It is for this reason that I began teaching mindfulness to individuals with autism.

A fuller discussion of those methods and observed results will come in later chapters.

For now, the takeaway from our discussion of the brain and trauma should be that trauma creates a shutdown of the logical, reasoning part of the brain and creates a default to an emotion-based reaction triggering our fight-or-flight response. This is what we want to keep in mind as we move into the next few chapters and begin our discussion of how the brain is affected by autism and how that becomes a trauma experience in individuals struggling with the disorder.

Chapter 3: The Autistic Brain and Sensory Trauma

I would like to move on to the discussion of what happens in the development of the autistic brain. First, let's discuss the structures in the brain that show a significant difference. We will start with the amygdala because, as we have seen, it is at the core of the fear response which triggers fight-or-flight. In many individuals with autism, it seems, the amygdala is larger and denser than in neurotypical individuals (Chen, Jiao, & Herskovits, 2011), (Schumann, Barnes, Lord, & Courchesne, 2009). This means that the autistic brain would be more responsive to sensory data it sees as potentially dangerous. Research indicates that children with ASD show an increase in anxiety chemicals (cortisol particularly) in response to stressors (Spratt, et al., 2011), triggering more quickly and intensely than in the neurotypical population.

In addition to the difference in the structure of the amygdala, there is evidence of an overall increase in brain size and a significant decrease in the corpus callosum (refer again to figure 2.1), (Chen, et.al., 2011). The corpus callosum is the communication bridge of the brain. It allows the whole brain to communicate and fully integrate information coming in and being stored. Remember here our discussion in the previous chapter about how the brain processes trauma memory by time-stamping it and attaching emotion, etc., to it and we can see how an underdeveloped corpus could affect this processing.

Add to this the evidence now being shown that early in life, the pruning of the brain in individuals with autism is very inefficient and that the brain is "over-connected," in a sense, and we can see how the delay in processing could be greatly affected (Tang, et al., 2014).

Let's look at how this brain is likely to work in a more, or less, integrated way. Sensory issues are a huge part of autism. One of the largest studies of the connectivity of the autistic brain to come out yet, as reported in *Frontiers in Neuroanatomy*, showed that the white matter of the autistic brain is much different than that in the neurotypical brain. In some regions (primarily the posterior cerebral region, which regulates sensory processing), it is severely underdeveloped, especially in boys (Chang, et al., 2016). So, already we have a part of the brain that is likely to have difficulty making sense of incoming sensory data.

If we consider the previously mentioned lack of neural pruning in the autistic brain, we begin to put the picture of the over-reactive mind together. In high-functioning individuals, pruning begins to catch up in adolescence and adulthood, which may explain why, in some cases, sensory issues seem to drop off after puberty (although not nearly in every individual does this happen). The unpruned brain becomes confused when trying to make sense of sensory input. In fact, the white matter of the brain is made mostly of these unpruned neural connections, and as reported above, is severely underdeveloped, often too dense or poorly formed and damaged (Chang, et al., 2016).

It is interesting to note here, that we see many of these same neurodevelopmental issues and deficiencies in the brains of young children who have endured extensive trauma.

So how is the brain to react when sensory input is sent from the thalamus to be processed? What does the amygdala infer when there is difficulty in making sense of it within the white matter? Remember our discussion above that the amygdala is often enlarged and denser than in the neurotypical brain. It is primed already to be triggered by this confusion and is ready to interpret it as a threat and err on the side of safety. Remember a time when your senses were not helpful to you? Perhaps you could not hear, or you were in a dark room where you could not see. It took a long time to sort out the sensory input and it was confusing. It was also probably frightening. Now multiply that experience by a hundred-fold. Fight-or-flight follows rapidly, cortisol levels and adrenalin levels spike and the meltdown goes from 0 to 60 in no time.

Peter Levine speaks at length about the "false positives" of the limbic brain meant to keep us safe. For instance, if I assume the rustling in the bushes behind me is a rabbit and I turn around to find it is a tiger, I could well be killed by the large predator. If, however, I assume it is a tiger and turn around to find it is only a rabbit, no harm will come to me. For this reason, the brain is wired to assume that information I can't make sense of must be dangerous (Levine & Van der Kolk, 2015).

In addition to this priming towards false positive responses, we find that cortisol levels in individuals with autism are already higher, so the spike causes a considerable response in the fight-or-flight system and meltdown results in an even more profound shutdown of the frontal lobe and rational thinking (Corbett & Simon, 2013), (Spratt, et al., 2011).

Let us revisit our discussion of PTSD in the light of the autistic brain. In the previous chapter, we discussed how a war veteran might react to the stimulus provided by fireworks with a fight-or-flight response based on the explosion triggering memories of combat. In the same way, individuals with strong sensory issues may seemingly become irrational and aggressive, or go into "elopement mode" for no apparent reason when, in fact, they are responding to some sensory trigger. For instance, I remember hearing the story of one individual who was terrified of fans. He would go into instant meltdown on just seeing one. This was because at one time, he had been in the room with a metal fan when the blades came loose and began banging loudly against the metal cage. He described the event as both terrifying and painful because of auditory sensory issues. The trauma of that instance created a very real trigger and fight-or-flight response in the brain anytime he saw a fan. The neurons for fan and painful auditory sensation had been wired together and the PTSD response was very real.

Peter Levine, in his book *Trauma and Memory*, talks about the process of memory storage. When we see objects that relate to past trauma, we don't simply take a snapshot of a fan and then store it neatly. We see the fan, process it through the memory we have of previous fans and what that means, and then respond and store the memory (Levine & Van der Kolk, 2015). So, the fan, when seen, immediately triggers prior memories of a fan and all the emotion and pain that entails. This, in turn, triggers the limbic fight-or-flight response.

There are multiple other cases of this trauma experience and we will discuss them in the chapter on sensory issues. What I want to convey here is that the brain wires together this painful sensory experience with the stimulus the thalamus is recording around the individual. Metal fan equals loud noise, equals pain, and the brain reacts to the sight of the metal fan, triggering a fight-or-flight safety response.

Chapter 4: The Trauma Effects of Autism

The point of the prior two chapters has been to set the stage and introduce you to how the brain of individuals on the spectrum is primed to respond to the environment much differently. Now I would like to look at the two major, and very real, ways that autism creates a trauma in the lives of individuals. The first is sensory overload and the second is a social form of trauma. Both are very real and have very real consequences in the lives of individuals.

Sensory Overload, the Over-Wired Brain and Trauma

What if every time a drop of water fell on your skin it felt like a burning ember? What if water felt gooey and green and cold and you could feel every drop as it ran along your skin? Would you shower often? Would your parents have to fight you to get you in the shower? I have known several individuals with this very experience.

Some individuals with autism experience "sensory overload," meaning that the sensory input simply cannot be filtered out and becomes too much to handle. Aaron Likens, author of the book *Finding Kansas: Living and Decoding Asperger's Syndrome,* described it in a lecture I saw him present as "living life unfiltered." He spoke about being unable to filter out distractions the way most individuals could and mentioned that when his sensory issues got bad, it felt like his skin was on fire (Likens, 2012).

Wendy Lampen gave a Ted talk on her experience with Asperger's syndrome and she talked about water running down her skin feeling like it was "old rose pink, gooey, dense stuff." Later in the talk, we see her struggle to find her words in a presentation she has probably practiced a thousand times because of the sound of a vacuum cleaner and discussion of the color yellow, which makes her physically sick (Lampen, 2012).

Synesthesia is a common experience in autism. It is the experience of having sensory input mixed up. Sound may generate colors, or numbers may have a taste. This is a result of sensory input being mixed up in the brain where there is too much wiring. I have listened to individuals explain that they bang their heads on the wall because it creates a distraction from other pain they are feeling or the pressure they feel in their heads. Again and again, we see how the sensory issues become confusing and even physically painful experiences. Synesthesia can also occur with Sensory Processing Disorder.

In other individuals, the sensory issues seem to keep putting pressure on them relentlessly until they find a way to meet the need and calm the stimulus from sensory input. Stimming is a series of repetitive physical motions or verbalizations that are meant to self-soothe. Often, stimming will include obsessive behaviors such as organizing objects in a way that mimics obsessive compulsive behavior. Sensory-seeking can also be a form of stimming at times. I have known individuals to stim on rapidly repeating music patterns or video and light patterns. In both cases, the input that is sought soothes the panicked brain because it is predictable and, therefore, comforting.

This same behavior is often seen in trauma victims who will rock to self-soothe, exhibit stimming type behaviors that are an expression of the anxiety they are experiencing, or self-harm to simply distract from the emotional pain. As I worked through my master's degree and dug deeper into trauma research, I began to recognize much of what I was seeing in my clients on the spectrum.

In both cases, the attempt is to still the storming brain and bring some sense of safety and comfort in a world that often seems terrifying. In the case of autism, as we saw in Chapter 3, the brain is primed for this trauma response. Confusion does not feel safe. Think of a situation where you were in a strange, unknown environment and felt lost. You did not know your way out and the anxiety started to increase. As the confusion builds, the heart rate goes up and a feeling of panic ensues. With an amygdala that is larger and denser, this reaction is strengthened and quickened.

This is the world of sensory confusion that individuals with autism face every day in some cases. Remember our discussion of the over-connectedness of the brain and how the white matter develops in a way that makes it difficult to navigate sensory input? It leaves the individual lost and confused in the sensory world around them. They are in a heightened state of alert already because of this, and the experience can become traumatic, even without additional painful stimulus.

Research is showing that it is not the big car crash, war or physical assault that creates the greatest traumas in the brain. These are all examples of "Big-T" traumas. What we are finding is that repeated stress over great time has a drip, drip, drip effect and creates complex trauma. These are "Little-T" traumas that shape the brain in significant ways much like autism. The reason is that these sensory issues begin to be a constant, corrosive force on the brain and create the trauma effects the same as daily neglect or criticism does in a child's life.

The Pariah Effect: Social Exclusion and Bullying as a Trauma Event

Now we come to the second form of trauma experienced in individuals with autism. This form of trauma, as we will see, is worst in high-functioning individuals and, unfortunately, not at all uncommon. This trauma is the trauma of social disconnection and isolation driven by repeated experiences of social exclusion or outright bullying. Even rejection, which is common and a normal part of developing relationship skills, can become traumatic for individuals on the spectrum because the seeming inability to "get it" socially becomes a repetitive trauma underlying that social growth spurt.

For just a second, we return to the brain of the individual with autism for exploration. The human brain is wired for social connection and functions best when it is being fed through this connection. One of the major chemicals the brain uses for social connection is oxytocin. It is the chemical that is secreted when mothers give birth, when they breast feed or when we stare deeply in one another's eyes or give hugs lasting more than a few seconds. This drug increases our level of relaxation and relieves the stress, reducing the cortisol and adrenaline the brain can produce during moments of anxiety.

Recent research suggests that an increase in oxytocin may create growth in the hippocampus, the region responsible for memory storage (fig. 2.1). In a report from the journal *Nature Neuroscience*, mice who were given increased levels of oxytocin showed an increase in hippocampal growth (Monks, Lonstein, & Breedlove, 2003). Oxytocin is responsible for bonding and is noticeably lower in individuals on the spectrum. New research is indicating the effectiveness of an oxytocin nasal spray in children with autism (Yatawara, Einfeld, Hickie, Davenport, & Guastella, 2015), (Watanabe, et al., 2014).

In addition to oxytocin, there is also increasing evidence that vasopressin may be indicated in the perspective deficit (the inability to see the other side of an argument or to register social cues at times),

(Digitale, 2015), (Heinrichs, Dawans, & Domes, 2009).
It seems that both of these hormone chemicals may play
a very large role in the social deficits that become so
painful in high-functioning autism during adolescence
and young adulthood (Zink & Meyer-Lindenberg, 2012).

One of the things oxytocin does is create a
pleasure response when bonding occurs during its
release, which encourages us to take risks emotionally
and bond with others. So now consider that you are an
individual who has little of the chemical necessary to
create the desire for bonding socially (Szalavitz & Perry,
2010). For positive social interaction to occur, it is also
necessary for me to be able to take the perspective of the
other. This is essentially what the relational part of
relationship is all about. But the chemical necessary in
helping us do this, vasopressin, is also lacking. These
two chemical deficiencies and other factors play into a
brain that is not good at relating socially or seeing from
others' perspectives. In real terms, this means the child
has a very difficult time in relating to peers and often
becomes the one others avoid, or who is directly made

fun of or bullied in school. Research indicates that trauma is often worst when it is emotional or verbal and that bullying falls well within these patterns of emotional abuse and trauma, especially in adolescence (Carney, 2008). If the individual does decide to risk all of this, he is generally getting less of the oxytocin social reward than the neurotypical individual would. What makes us want to take the chance at being rejected is the feel-good payoff oxytocin gives us when it works, and if we are not getting that, our motivation is seriously reduced.

The trauma of social exclusion and bullying is very real. It is not uncommon in my practice to have patients in their mid to late 20's who still have few, if any, intimate friends, and no developed love interests, simply because the pain of past trauma has left them unwilling to risk vulnerability. When the individual has carved out a relatively comfortable existence for themselves with work, gaming, etc., then the risk of further emotional trauma is seldom something they are easily attracted to, even when the desire for a relationship is there. This social trauma and treatment is discussed further in later chapters.

Chapter 5: Sensory Issues, Sensory Integration and Sensory Diets

I think we can see now how trauma quickly becomes a part of the experience of autism. What we sometimes fail to realize, even as well-meaning professionals, is how that interferes with learning. I have had numerous conversations with educators, case managers and other professionals who deal with autism on a regular basis. Inevitably, I hear from many of them that they are frustrated by the fact that they are trying everything they can think of to teach this child. They are throwing behavioral services at them and none of it seems to work.

In one such instance, a case manager was speaking to me about a client who had been in an ABA services program for six months and they felt like he wasn't really learning anything. Behaviors had not changed and there was no real progress being made in school. I asked the case manager if there were any sensory issues. There were "a ton" of sensory issues.

Next question, "What's being done about them?"
Answer, "Not much." So, I gave the case manager an
example I use a lot in presentations and when talking to
professionals. "Let's say," I said, "I had a really
fascinating book about exactly the type of things you're
really interested in and I gave it to you and asked you to
read it. You are going to be given three minutes to read
what you can and then you will be quizzed over what
you have read. But, while you are reading, I am going to
slap you in the face with a wet towel every 10 seconds or
so. How will you do on the quiz?" His answer was,
"probably not so good."

    School counselors can tell you that trauma
interferes with learning. Distractions interfere with
learning. The reason we have school breakfast and lunch
provided is because we know that children cannot learn
if they are distracted by their hunger. This is based on
the work of Abraham Maslow, who realized that human
beings will not move on to higher needs like learning,
social attainment and even spiritual growth unless their
basic safety and security needs are met.

When a child is constantly under sensory assault, they have no real interest in learning. It is a traumatic experience. Research indicates that children with sensory integration issues experience both behavioral control and learning difficulties. It has even been found that auditory sensory issues cause far more problems with behavior and learning than other sensory issues (Ashburner, Ziviani, & Rodger, 2008). I strongly suspect this is a matter of auditory sensory issues being far more distracting, difficult to filter out and producing a stronger trauma effect. Whatever the causative case may be, we see clearly how sensory issues can and do interfere with learning and create trauma.

Types of Sensory Issues

Before we get started, I want the reader to understand that I am not an Occupational or Physical Therapist (OT/PT) and what I am discussing here is what I have learned from workshops and research along those lines. The suggestions I am making here and the assessment list I have created are based on that knowledge and I encourage you to begin with that. I also encourage you to find a good OT/PT and get a full assessment done along with sensory integration work, which we will discuss later. I would like the reader to take from this discussion a strong idea of what sensory issues are, what types the individual might be struggling with and some basic suggestions about where to begin with treatment at home.

Now let's look at how sensory issues are divided into categories and what that means experientially and for treatment. Individuals can be either hypersensitive to sensory issues (over-reactive to input) or hypo-sensitive (under-reactive to input). We will start with the under-reactive type, which can be divided into two categories.

First, there are the individuals who are under-responsive to sensory input over all. They may seem very low energy, very flat in affect and not very responsive to anything. In schools, they are often the kids who simply don't seem motivated or excited by any activities because the sensory input that would excite most of us is simply not registering. They may not register physical touch, they may not feel temperature extremes or even pain. Some individuals have such a high pain threshold that bath water must be monitored or they will step into a scalding bath and get second-degree burns without ever responding to sensation. These same individuals may not be able to distinguish taste or smells. They may have little sense of where their body is located in space and seem very clumsy at times. Roller coasters may not thrill them, they may not show fear when perching in high, dangerous places. In some cases, they may have issues with incontinence because they cannot feel the bladder pressure and can't tell when they must go to the bathroom.

Many of the symptoms of the under-responsive individual are also seen in trauma survivors. This is because in cases of extreme trauma, survivors cut themselves off from body awareness that could trigger trauma memory and sensation. They literally numb out, and this can look a lot like autism in children and adolescents. This is because the brain responds in much the same way to the trauma whether it is caused by others or the environment. Dissociation becomes a coping mechanism for these individuals.

Now let's look at the under-reactive individuals known as sensory-seekers. In much the same way, they are not responding to sensory input, but there is a craving for that input in many individuals. It is not entirely understood why this happens, but it is my suspicion that the sensory-seeking behavior is feeding their brain in a way that calms and centers them in the midst of a very confusing world. It is, in many ways, a form of neurological stimming. These individuals are often labeled as ADHD when the sensory-seeking behavior is mistaken for a lack of attention. They may stand under a chandelier and tap it to see it sparkle or be fascinated by fans or pinwheels. They may seek out certain sounds repetitively or want constantly to be stroked, scratched or touched in some way. They may crave sour or spicy foods. All of these things would indicate sensory-seeking and in some cases, the seeking behavior can be dangerous—especially when combined with the occasional lack of fear that can result from under-responsivity. This is why we occasionally hear of a young man or woman who has wandered off from home, gone to the neighbor's pool and because they are fascinated by water, jumped in even though they cannot swim.

In cases like these, it becomes very important that we begin finding ways to meet the sensory needs that are structured and safe. In fact, when we do help individuals meet these sensory needs, the research shows they are able to focus and return to the task at hand with more retention and understanding. If we return to the wet towel example, we can see why.

Tommy, an 8-year-old boy I worked with, had become fascinated by fire and other dangerous sensations that made it necessary for him to be monitored around the clock because he would seldom sleep. One of the needs he expressed was hearing the sound of sizzling. He would take hand towels from wherever he could find them, run water from the sink over them and put them in the waffle iron. He was extremely intelligent, and when mom decided to lock up the towels in a closet so he could not gain access, he decided to take off his underwear and use that. He was a problem-solver, if nothing else.

In a meeting with his mental health team, it was initially believed this was just oppositional, attention-seeking behavior. All behavior, however, is an attempt to communicate something, and while some of it may have been attention-seeking, the behaviors being exhibited were very sensory-involved. It was hypothesized that this was a calming experience for him, a stimming behavior of sorts. I suggested that gentle rain falling sounded a lot like sizzling bacon so we should find one of the nighttime background noise makers that produce the sound of rain. Mom said that his sister had one and he had played with it so much that he had worn it out. Mom had simply not put together that this behavior was an attempt to calm the storm in his mind. None of us had, until that moment.

Eventually, Thomas increased his behaviors to the point that they were again becoming dangerous. His mom was getting no sleep, and it was simply impossible to keep up the pace. Thomas was entered into a residential placement arrangement where he lived in an apartment with 24-hour staff who could provide around-the-clock structure and give him undivided attention (not possible if you are a working mom with kids). The process was hard for mom, but she was a trooper who showed every day that she was willing to do anything to see that Thomas was well cared for. Within a few months, Thomas had adjusted to the new environment, all his sensory needs were being met and his medication regimen had been adjusted. His behaviors reduced to nearly zero, he started doing well in school, and mom, initially very stressed over her choice, has her boy back and is bonding with him in ways that would have not been possible previously.

Thomas is an extreme example, but his story illustrates both the importance of meeting sensory needs and how difficult it can be to recognize what is going on. This is a very real struggle for parents.

Now let's look at hypersensitivity to sensory input. These individuals find it extremely difficult to filter out or make sense of sensory input. Neurotypical students may hear a neighbor tapping a pencil against a desk during class and can filter out that noise in favor of the lecture they are hearing, but individuals with hypersensitivity often cannot. This is what Aaron

Likens meant when he talked about "living life unfiltered" (Likens, 2012). Recall our discussion of speaker Wendy Lampen who lost track of her words just from hearing the sound of a vacuum cleaner in the midst of a talk she had, no doubt, practiced hundreds of times.

John was an individual who was so sensitive to sound that the world had become very unsafe to him. High-functioning and undiagnosed until late adolescence, he fell in with the wrong crowd and they introduced him to drugs. It wasn't long before he was using IV heroin and methamphetamine to escape the sensory overload. When John's mother called, she was in tears; he was 22, homeless and using IV drugs. She was terrified. We got John admitted to a rehab, but rehabs in the U.S. are group-oriented and he was pacing and not making eye contact. The case manager wanted him out of the program because she felt he was not paying attention. I assured her that even though he was pacing, he was listening to every word and he would eventually have questions about the discussion after he had been given the necessary time for processing. She would not hear it and he was released to his parents. He went home to live with them and we set a meeting.

John's parents are good people. They were simply lost and had no clue about the sensory issues John was dealing with or the trauma they were creating. They had been given little information after the diagnosis. When we talked about his hearing sensitivity, it came out that he could hear the powerlines buzzing outside the duplex with doors and windows closed. This was not the first person I had known who could hear powerlines buzzing. Trips to busy stores where there was noise and crowds were out of the question. We discussed some options for dealing with the sensory issues, including mindfulness practice as a way of filtering the issues out and making the reduction of those issues the number one goal.

I had a deal with John that if he made the one-year-clean mark, I would take him for a dinner of his choice. I talked with John's mother just before beginning this book. I still owe him that dinner and the offer still stands. It has been three years since John used any drugs. He is prescribed Suboxone to help with the opiate addiction but has not used street drugs to cope with the sensory assault since that meeting.

John's story is not uncommon. I have treated many addicts who were also either on the spectrum, diagnosed with ADHD or both. Many of them started with prescribed psychostimulants and graduated to the more powerful methamphetamine along the way. I have successfully helped many of them control the symptoms of ADHD without the use of psychostimulants so that they were able to stay clean and not relapse. Mindfulness training has been the key component in every case, and we will get to how that is trained in a later chapter. For now, it's enough to know that it works.

The trauma of sensory issues is very real, as we have seen. They bombard the autistic brain that cannot process or make sense of them quickly and create confusion, synesthesia and very real physical pain, at times. The extra time creates a marked decrease in executive functioning (the ability to move from one task to another smoothly and without confusion), which further interferes with learning in schools. Individuals will find ways to account for this trauma. Some of these ways will be behaviors that seem oppositional or simply odd. But every behavior is a communication to us about what is going on within that over-connected brain. We simply have to listen and keep asking what it is that will make them feel safe.

Sensory Assessments and Diets

One way we can begin listening is with a sensory assessment. In appendix A, you will find a brief assessment of sensory needs that is fairly simple to use. The idea is to get a general overview of where the needs are and how they are expressing themselves. The sensory issues are divided into six key areas. They are:

1. Tactile (touch)
2. Proprioceptive (body in space and depth perception)
3. Vestibular (inner ear and balance)
4. Vision
5. Auditory
6. Taste and Smell

The major senses are self-explanatory, but I would like to discuss what proprioceptive and vestibular issues are in more depth, since many have not heard of them.

Proprioception is concerned with the body in space. Essentially, it is knowing where I stop and the rest of the world starts. Individuals with proprioception issues may have boundary issues and invade personal space, seem clumsy or have depth-perception issues. It is not uncommon for them to not like tile patterns that change because they cannot judge the depth, or to have real fear of escalators for the same reason.

Daniel was a young man with moderate to high-functioning autism and mild cognitive deficits. He was very sweet and terrified of escalators. He would not go near them. In the shopping center we visited when I worked with him, there were escalators and large checker-tiled floors. He would only walk on the white squares because he could not tell how deep the black tiles were. We began a program of desensitization. We moved very slowly. He trusted me, and we began with him just watching me ride up and down. Then he would feel the hand rail slide between his fingers. Then after about six months of going once a week, he actually rode the escalator. Once he defeated the demon, it was all he wanted to do nearly every time I worked with him after that. The desensitization was only part of the battle. Winning his trust was far more important. If he trusted me, he feared less and was willing to struggle on through the issues to learn how to account for them. It all began by simply noticing what his behavior was telling me about why he did not feel safe.

Vestibular issues are inner ear type problems. Not too many years ago, I had a Black Lab by the name of Hank that worked with me as a therapy dog. As Hank got older, there was a time that he would shake his head and could not stand up. I was terrified he had a tumor. I called the vet and the vet said it was not uncommon for labs to have vestibular disease. Based on my work in autism, I knew what Hank needed. I put him in a rocker that spun and spun him round and round for five minutes. I don't think Hank enjoyed the ride much, but he could walk when we were done. Vestibular issues will be most evident when the child likes spinning in circles or watching spinning wheels that would make most of us dizzy, bouncing on trampolines, hanging upside down, rocking his head from side to side or in a "no" motion. These are all indicators that there could be vestibular issues.

The sensory assessment list in appendix A can be used to make a cursory evaluation of these issues and the cited websites there can be used to get an idea of helpful activities. However, this should only be seen as a start and a good OT is an invaluable source for getting at the root of the sensory issues and honing in on the supports that will be most helpful. I strongly recommend getting your child assessed by a certified OT/PT. As mentioned before, there is a great deal of research indicating that if we begin treating the sensory issues effectively, the behavioral issues lessen or go away entirely.

Sensory Integration and Brain Development

Another support we can provide in helping to account for the sensory issues is sensory integration work. Remember that we mentioned one way the brain in autism differs from NT's (NeuroTypicals) is that the corpus callosum is underdeveloped and the brain is primed for trauma response. The brain suffering from trauma does not process well. As discussed, the amygdala short circuits the processing and cuts out the top half of the brain to save time and react more quickly to perceived dangers. The brain naturally processes from bottom to top and from right to left. When treating trauma, part of treatment is recalling the trauma and keeping the client engaged in processing through the whole brain. This is the power of EMDR, brain spotting and mindfulness. We integrate processing bottom to top and right to left, creating a whole brain experience.

Sensory integration works in much the same way by pushing processing on a whole-brain level. Many OT's will do exercises that involve crossing the midline, like playing patty cake, or tapping on the opposite shoulders with your right and left hands. This begins to integrate left-right processing of the brain. In addition, we could have music on in the background which begins to activate the brain on a whole-brain auditory level. Finally, research is indicating that essential oils can trigger the release of "feel good" brain chemicals like serotonin (Komiya, Takeuchi, & Harada, 2006). The point here is that we are gently activating the whole brain in processing activities.

This sensory integration work is proving to be very powerful in rewiring the brain (Pfeiffer, Koenig, Kinnealey, Sheppard, & Henderson, 2011), (Schaaf, 2010). In fact, research in the area of trauma and PTSD shows that sensory integration is an effective treatment for those issues as well (Kaiser, Gillette, & Spinazzola, 2010). This makes sense, considering our discussion earlier about the brain functioning of trauma survivors and how it resembles the functioning of the brain with autism. Repeatedly I experience clients who have survived trauma and exhibit stimming behaviors like rocking. In addition, they will at times become dissociative to the point that they are not able to verbalize what they are experiencing. Were they still experiencing the actual trauma they had survived or other stressors on a regular basis, this withdrawal could easily become more permanent, which is exactly what we see in autism.

The point that I would like the reader to leave the discussion of sensory issues with is the very real trauma that they induce. This trauma resembles in nearly every way the trauma that abuse victims suffer. The one major difference is that professionals try and teach children with autism how to manage behaviors and develop new social skills while they are still being assaulted by the environment. Any trauma therapist will tell you that a child being abused is almost impossible to help until she is taken out of the traumatic environment or that environment is changed. Teaching her to "behave" better would make no sense in those conditions. Trauma management and treatment comes first, and then we teach new coping and behavioral skills.

Chapter 6: The Use of Mindfulness Training

Mindfulness is simply focusing on one thing in one moment to calm the mind and keep the attention from wandering. It is a powerful tool in the treatment of anxiety, trauma, depression and PTSD. That is why I began using it specifically in the treatment of autism, and it has been equally as powerful there. I will begin this section with a general discussion of mindfulness, its effect on the brain and brain chemistry and the results it produces in the neurotypical population. From there, I will move on to how I came to believe it would work with autism and the results my practice has shown. Finally, we will look at methods briefly and how they vary depending on age and level of intellectual functioning.

The Use of Mindfulness in the Treatment of Trauma

Recall our earlier discussion of the brain's reaction in moments of trauma. The amygdala is triggered and creates a fight-or-flight response, causing the secretion of cortisol and adrenaline. The body reacts by increasing heart rate and respiration while tensing muscles and getting ready to spring into action. The body and brain can be said to be one unit at this point. In fact, in the treatment of trauma, we often talk about top-down and bottom-up processing. Top-down is from the brain to the body while bottom-up is from the body back to the brain in the loop of brain-body connection.

Generally, when we think about the body, we think of it as being controlled by the brain. The truth, however, is more complex. The body can trigger the brain into responding as well. This is where mindfulness comes in. When we feel stress and tension, we can change the panicked brain by beginning to control the body. In fact, research indicates that individuals who learn mindfulness stress reduction techniques lower the levels of cortisol in their bodies and brains (Daubenmier, Hayden, Chang, & Epel, 2014), (Mccomb, Tacon, Randolph, & Caldera, 2004). This brain-body connection goes both ways, and we can slow the body by controlling and regulating breathing to calm the anxious and triggered brain.

In mid 2015, I had to have a stress test on my heart. Essentially, they put the patient on a treadmill and run them like a gerbil in a wheel until the heart hits a target rate while measuring its reactions to the stress. Unless, like me, you have severe arthritis in your knees that makes you a fall risk in such situations. In that case, they do a chemical stress test. If you are ever given the option between the treadmill and the chemical stress test, I advise the treadmill. In fact, if you are given a choice between being attacked by an angry gorilla and a chemical stress test, I'm pretty sure the gorilla is the better option. It was not fun. Essentially, they inject a chemical into your veins to run your heart rate up. My target rate was 155 beats per minute. The brain reacts to this heart rate by beginning to panic. The body is telling it that there must be something horribly wrong by bringing up the heart rate that high. I could feel the fight-or-flight, anxiety response begin in my brain. The science geek side of me thought "This is fascinating!" The human side of me was not so fond of the experience at all. So, I did what I do when I feel anxiety…I began to monitor and slow my breathing. My mind began to calm and the heartrate went from 145 to 135 beats per minute. The nurses were not happy about this and made me stop, but the point we take from this experience is that the body-brain connection is bi-directional and very real.

Mindfulness is that simple.

It's a matter of watching the breath and becoming the observer of our mind and emotions rather than following them down any rabbit holes. The point of mindfulness is to allow our thoughts and emotions simply to be and release their control over us. It is not to control our thoughts and emotions. That is an exercise in futility. Thoughts and emotions will come whether we want them to or not. The point is to keep our thoughts and emotions from controlling us, from determining our behavior.

Anxiety, PTSD and trauma responses can be released in much the same way simply by controlling the breath and focusing on the gentle rise and fall of our chests as we fill our lungs and then exhale. This is, in fact, where and how I begin teaching mindfulness to patients. Simply by breathing in and out and counting to three slowly and silently on the inhale, holding for a two-count, then breathing out to a silent count of three. This creates a regulated pattern of breathing that controls the body function and tells the anxious brain that everything is, in fact, okay.

Another facet of mindfulness is teaching individuals to become aware of anxiety as it rises in the body. So, we spend lots of time in session checking in with the body to see where the tension is when we are discussing difficult and traumatic memories. In this way, the individual becomes aware of when and where they start to tense up when anxiety is setting in. By doing this, we create an early warning signal and it becomes second nature for them to begin regulating the breathing as soon as they feel the tension start. Add this to daily practice during times when we are not stressed, and the brain begins to change its neural patterns and connections. It begins to break the over-reactive attachments and rewire in such a way that our response to stress becomes regulated breathing.

Anxiety is fear that is almost always rooted in the future or the past. It is a fear of what has happened replaying in the present or a fear of what might happen in the future that triggers the anxiety response in many cases. In the instances where this anxiety is on the verge of becoming a full-blown panic, I recommend using a grounding exercise. This exercise is simply taking two of the regulated breaths I described and then looking around and naming quietly to oneself three things that can be seen, then taking two more breaths and listening for three things that can be heard, then taking two final regulating breaths. It is nearly impossible for us to be focused on what is in our present and what is in our future or past. This exercise is very good at rooting us in the here and now and using the body and the senses to tell the brain we are all right and there is no need for panic. It releases the fear by grounding us firmly in the safety of the present.

In my work with trauma patients, I have had a lot of success using these techniques in controlling anxiety and panic. It was my own success with these techniques and my research in their use with trauma that led me to believe they could be easily adapted to be used with autism. In fact, in many instances I saw therapists and behavioral staff using breathing exercises to try and stave off meltdown mode but using them in a crisis is often less than effective, depending on the method. But now that we've looked at how mindfulness can help calm the brain in neurotypical individuals, let's look at how it can, and does, work with individuals on the spectrum.

Mindfulness and the Autistic Brain

In 2013, I began to research mindfulness and trauma. Before long, I became convinced this could work with autism too and began looking for research there. There was little to no research. I called several of the major autism treatment centers in the Midwest and there was nothing. In conversation with a lead therapist for one of the largest outfits in Missouri, it became obvious they did not even know what mindfulness was. I asked if they used any breathing techniques and they said, "Oh yeah, we do some of that." This was the extent of mindfulness as it was being used then.

What I did find in my research was proof that mindfulness could do wonderful things like reduce cortisol, increase oxytocin, regulate emotional states and change emotionally reactive responses (Howard & Howard, 2007), (Mccomb, et.al., 2004), (Daubenmier, et. al., 2014), (Van der Kolk, 2014), (Young, 2011), (Brand, Holsboer-Trachsler, Naranjo, & Schmidt, 2012),

(Kim, et al., 2013). I also found research indicating that Cognitive Behavioral Therapy interventions worked as well with patients on the high-functioning end of the spectrum (Sofronoff, Attwood, Hinton, & Levin, 2006) which led me to believe that more advanced mindfulness would also work. We will get into specific techniques later in this chapter, but for now, it is sufficient to say that some forms of mindfulness/meditation require imagination and the ability to think abstractly more than others and it was these more advanced methods that I was often using at this point in the treatment of trauma and addictions.

Essentially, I had come to believe that if mindfulness works in the neurotypical population, it should work for individuals on the high-functioning end of the spectrum. I came to this conclusion as a result of evidence pointing to the fact that cognitive therapies worked for high functioning autism (HFA). If we consider the trauma response of the autistic brain discussed in chapter 3 and the chemical responses that resemble the brain affected by trauma, we begin to see how mindfulness can work. Certainly, it works with trauma and therefore should work as well with the trauma due to autism.

What I found in the research strengthened this belief and went well beyond just the control of trauma. The research was showing that mindfulness helped improve brain functioning in other ways that would greatly aid in the treatment of autism. In a study of available research by Kirk, Fatola and Gonzalez, there was strong evidence that mindfulness increased the functioning of the developing regions of the brain in adolescents and an increase in executive functioning, which is one of the key problems with individuals struggling with HFA. The same review of research found that the activation of the limbic region (the fight-or-flight, trauma response system) was considerably lowered (Kirk, Fatola, & Gonzalez, 2016). Essentially, this means that individuals are able to keep the front part of the brain online long enough to make better, more reasoned decisions in the world instead of simply reacting to it.

We see this often in schools when children are asked to switch from one subject or activity to another.

The child is very high-functioning and exhibits no apparent cognitive disability and so they do not show the need for an IEP as reflected in testing. The problem here is that one of the primary difficulties presented with autism is the problem of executive functioning. Remember from our earlier conversation that executive functioning is, in large part, the ability to switch smoothly from one subject to another without a lot of confusion or break down complex tasks quickly into component steps. Because the brain is over-connected, this involves a lot more sorting for kids on the spectrum. It simply takes longer to process the new task instructions, which is why kids with autism do much better when tasks are broken into smaller pieces.

Because we have seen that mindfulness assists in neural pruning, we would expect then that executive functioning might also improve as a result of having fewer connections to navigate. In fact, research shows that the increase of executive functioning is indeed one of the results of mindfulness practice (Teper & Inzlicht, 2012). Mindfulness assists in the pruning of the brain and allows for the child to create an emotional space for just a few seconds (the length of one breath), enabling her to turn off the emotionally reactive limbic region, allowing time for the executive decision-making process to complete.

Case Studies in Mindfulness

I have seen mindfulness in my own practice have a huge impact on emotional control. The techniques used will vary depending on age, cognitive ability and presenting issues but there is almost always a way to teach mindfulness at every level of cognitive functioning. If I am working with an individual that is 12 but has an IQ north of 140, he is probably more capable than the average 12-year-old of grasping abstract concepts, so I will use more advanced techniques for him. If, however, my client is 30 but she is showing cognitive deficits or severe sensory issues that are interfering with cognitive processing, then the methods need to be more concrete and less abstract. A few examples follow:

"Daniel" is a 20-year-old male who was having issues with meltdown and severe aggression against even people he loved. In meltdown mode, he would become so dysregulated that he would destroy property, physically assault his mother and become suicidal. At one point, he was running into the highway and laying down hoping to be hit by oncoming traffic. He found it nearly impossible to be in crowds of people. We initially explored sensory issues and found that he was very sensitive to auditory issues and to crowds, which made him nervous. His anxiety level was through the roof. In addition, he had trauma from bullying in his school years that made him very reactive (this kind of trauma will be covered in the chapter on social adjustment and trauma).

I began teaching him two forms of mindfulness exercise. The first was what most people think of when they think of mindfulness. It was simply cyclical breathing and paying attention to the body. Basic relaxation meditation. But one thing I noticed about Daniel was that when he was anxious, he would roll a small ball with nodules on it in his fingers. The tactile input seemed to be calming his anxious brain. This became our point of focus for another exercise in mindfulness to teach filtering of the outer world. It is an extension of what many people already do when they disappear into a game or book. They are filtering out the anxious world around them and immersing themselves into a more controllable and safer world.

For this exercise, we took the blue ball that had become a point of focus already and made exploring it a very conscious activity. We noticed its color, how densely patterned the nodules were, how it felt as we rolled it between our fingers. We took a full five minutes just focusing on the sensory input this ball had to offer. We made sure to regulate the breathing during this observational exercise. Daniel noticed he was much calmer after this activity. Then I suggested the next time he was in a stressful environment, like at Target, he take the ball with him and roll it between his fingers while it was in his pocket. Really focusing on it like we had in the exercise. Daniel no longer has issues with being in public. There have been no instances of suicidal behavior. In fact, he is now employed part time in the community. He is now able to manage without the meltdowns resulting in aggression and attempted self-harm. In just over a year, he has experienced these significant changes because we began dealing with both the sensory trauma and trauma that he had suffered in school from bullying. We will discuss the trauma of social exclusion in a later chapter and return to Daniel.

Jimmy was an eight-year-old boy who had progressed normally in his development of verbal skills until he was five. At age five, the sensory issues increased greatly (this is not uncommon it seems when growth and hormonal changes occur) and he became entirely nonverbal and extremely agitated and aggressive. When I began working with him, his mother was very angry and had little faith I was going to be able to help either. She reported to me that they had an ABA specialist in there to help and she had mostly "Spent her time restraining him every day while he kicked and yelled and bit her." I inquired what had been done in the way of a sensory assessment and diet. There was no indication much was being done in the home at that time, which, mom explained, was due in part to apartment management having issues with anything hanging on walls or ceilings. The school had made some effort and noticed progress. So, for Jimmy, I felt that we first needed to implement a good sensory world and then work on mindfulness to teach him to cope with remaining stressors and focus through the noise. We integrated with the school about sensory issues and what they were seeing and contacted apartment management about ADA compliance.

My first several sessions were not interactive at all. I simply watched him as he played around us and mom and I discussed his sensory issues and created a profile. The extent of his involvement was my watching him hang upside down in contorted positions on the couch and mentioning what a limber monkey he was, which would elicit a giggle. Towards the end of the second session as we discussed what I felt was needed for equipment in the home, he came very close to me and sat down. Mom was obviously nervous, having pried him off of previous therapists mid-assault. He simply ran his hand gently up my arm. It was his way of saying

I was safe and my cue to begin the next phase of work with him.

We began working on mindfulness practice. Jimmy was very fond of food and gummies were his absolute favorite, so we began there. I took a bag of gummies (six in a pack) and we began exploring them. We looked at the shape, how they felt rolling between our fingers, whether they were hard or soft, what color they were and what they smelled like. Finally, if he could verbally give me the actual color of the gummy, he could eat it. Our first time I got three colors out of six gummies verbally. The whole package and lots of cheering was his reward. We made his environment safer by letting him set his own pace and then we focused on filtering the environment to improve focus with the mindfulness exercise and the results were astounding.

I released Jimmy to another local therapist because he was very high energy and she specialized in a more kinetic sensory type of experience that I thought would benefit him. Two months later, mom left a comment on my business page:

> *Robert is the first provider to focus on my*
> *son's sensory needs as a primary treatment.*
> *Since we have implemented a sensory*
> *based therapeutic ideal, my son has made the*
> *most progress he has in years! He is no longer*
> *regressing, but PROgressing. And more*
> *importantly, I got my sweet good natured,*
> *FUNNY kid back!*

It reminded me of exactly why I love my work.

When we begin implementing the sensory diet, we begin to calm the anxious mind. From there, we can implement mindfulness to treat remaining anxiety and improve the ability to filter out the remaining environment. Using this direction of treatment, as we have seen, can greatly reduce or even end the need for behavioral services. I am working with families in increasing numbers who are at their wit's end and losing hope that their child will be able to function simply because they have been trying to teach her new skills when all she is interested in is stopping the assaultive world around her. I continue to see the positive results of using this trauma approach in family after family. We will cover methods for teaching some of these techniques in the chapter on treatment specifics.

Chapter 7: Autism in the School

I want to begin looking at autism in the schools. I have seen schools and educators who were extremely dedicated still struggling with kids on the spectrum because they simply were at a loss. Sadly, I have also seen schools that were simply focused on the bottom line, were not interested in thinking outside the box and simply tried to bully parents into home schooling their children. I have heard stories from parents that left me in shock. In one instance, I was in on a meeting for a four-year-old who was nonverbal and severely autistic. I became livid when one of the "professionals" at the school suggested this child could not learn and would not progress. One of the skills I have learned since is tact. I am afraid I did not possess that skill at that meeting and told the "professional" that if I could teach a therapy dog, I could teach this child. Six months later, she was making pre-verbal utterances, using sign language to indicate basic needs, feeding herself and assisting in bathing herself. None of these she was doing prior to that meeting. It is unfortunate, but not every teacher in the field is dedicated. Others I have known have amazing hearts and simply refuse to give up no matter the hours or the frustration.

It is not uncommon for me to hear from parents or the school counselors that the school has "tried everything" and simply doesn't know what to do anymore. Often, this is because they are using a playbook designed for "most" behavioral scenarios. But kids on the spectrum don't fit into any of the "most of the time" categories. They truly are each very individual in his/her needs because of the wide variety of sensory experiences that can be had. In many of the IEP's I have attended with parents we have been met with unprepared, but well-meaning teachers and school counselors who were used to looking at autism as a primarily behavioral problem. They are almost always creative, open to learning and simply lost. Team approaches in these instances are amazingly productive.

Again, treatment should involve a good OT assessment and begin with meeting sensory needs. Sensory breaks are generally more common and last longer the younger the child is. This happens for two reasons. First, and I believe foremost, is because as the child ages, they begin to adapt to the world around them and find ways to cope. It is a matter of survival for them that they do so. Second, we know that as children age, the brain continues to prune. The higher functioning the individual is, the more the pruning will begin to approach rates and levels of pruning that are on par with NTs (Tang, et al., 2014).

I should say that many schools do a very good job of integrating sensory breaks. Others, it seems, feel constrained by ever tightening budgets and "sensory equipment" can be very expensive. But anything can become sensory equipment. I work with parents all the time on a budget and instead of buying expensive sensory lighting, we go to Amazon and purchase monofilament lights that change color and allow the child to touch them and make wavy patterns, or blow up canoe chairs that become squeeze devices for a tenth of the price that we might pay at a specialist shop. Be creative, find ways to feed the need without breaking the bank. Included with the sensory checklist in the back of this book are links to suggested activities for various sensory needs. Find cheap ways to make that happen and you will find the payoff in learning and focus is huge.

High-Functioning Autism in Schools

Where I see most of the problem in schools is with adolescents who are very high-functioning. Cognitively they show no deficits and their grades may be very good in certain classes and bottom out in others. They may be having "tantrums" that people are perceiving as a resistance to doing work. Often, I have found that there are two or three things going on here. Again, it is related to that trauma primed brain and the response to expectations and the environment.

The most common issue I find is the failure to recognize that in high-functioning individuals we still often see problems with executive functioning. To review, executive functioning is the brain's ability to organize and order tasks so that switching from one task to another is less confusing and goes more smoothly. Often individuals with problems in this area find it much easier to accomplish tasks if they are broken down into a list of individual steps. As an example, tying one's shoes. Tying one's shoes consists of many steps that can be learned as a skill by watching. But for individuals on the spectrum and those with issues in executive functioning, it helps to break it down into very methodical steps:

1. Pick up right string in right hand
2. Pick up left string in left hand
3. Pull strings tight
4. Move strings to opposite hands
5. Cross strings and pull tight
6. Make loop in right string...

You get the point here. Many kids on the spectrum, even those with extremely high IQ's, do better with directions when they are broken into small pieces.

Most classrooms are not equipped with this level of instruction. Especially when the student gets to high school. It is often assumed then that there is a level of ability that may not exist in this area when it comes to breaking down tasks. So, when the teacher tells the 8th grader to put books away and pick up the computer, or to close the computer and go to the lab area, this takes more time to process. Often, because the student is so high-functioning, educators miss the fact that they still need the extra time to process the instructions and not following through is mistaken for resistance.

I have also known this to become an issue in reading and writing. The IQ may be through the roof but organizing the thoughts into a coherent paragraph becomes a struggle. Or reading comprehension may seem to be compromised when there is difficulty with transitions, making it difficult to put the story together. The bottom line is that the intelligence makes it difficult to see what is not working and the child is very adept at accounting for deficiencies.

Secondly, the child may have sensory issues that are not being seen clearly because they have learned to account for them in most instances. Many high-functioning individuals learn to hide those differences very quickly and begin adjusting to their environments the best they can, even though in more extreme circumstances (exceptionally loud or crowded environments) they may not be able to any longer.

Again, the fact that they are functioning at a high cognitive level mistakenly leads even school counselors to overlook the deeper issues caused by the autism. Following are two example case studies of this experience.

Luke is a nine-year-old whose IQ is well above 150. He was having constant meltdowns in class and would hide under desks to reduce the sensory input and would frequently simply refuse to do work that he could easily have finished. The response of staff was to order him out from under the desk, and when that did not happen, they used security to forcibly pull him from under the desk resulting in increased aggression and rug burns. When this was relayed to me by mom, I was a little shocked. They had done exactly the opposite of what was needed.

The school agreed to allow me to consult at the IEP meeting. Luke and I began working on some mindfulness exercises in the office and I made several recordings available for use at home and in school. The school agreed to several things. First, we would give Luke time to respond when he needed it. Second, if

Luke felt he needed a break to leave the class and separate from the noise and distraction, he would be allowed to go to the counselor's office to do so. Third, Luke would go to the counselor's office before the start of school each morning where he could listen to and practice the prerecorded mindfulness exercises with the school counselor and then again before or after lunch (his choice), he would return to practice with her again. When Luke got home he would use the recording at night to help him sleep because he was having nightmares that were keeping him up at night.

It was less than two weeks after implementing these supports that Luke went from daily instances of problem behavior to no problems at all. The school wrote to ask permission to begin using the meditations with other students they felt could be helped. His mother and grandparents reported huge, positive behavioral changes at home. After several months, and right before Christmas, I asked jokingly if Luke thought the fat man in the red suit was going to show up. He laughingly informed me he had been given the student of the month award at school and said, "Oh yeah, I think he's coming." I released him as a patient shortly after.

Tom is a 13-year-old student in 8th grade who is extremely high-functioning. He was showing an increase in aggressive behaviors verbally and then it escalated to physical aggression against another student who had been teasing him. Again, I attended the IEP meeting and we discussed implementing much of the same supports. I provided the school with mindfulness recordings that he could use and we trained in a grounding exercise that could be used when he felt the anger and anxiety beginning to rise in his body. It is the grounding exercise I commonly use with neurotypical patients who are coping with anxiety. Two regulated, mindful breaths followed by looking around the environment and saying quietly to themselves three things they see. Two more breaths followed by three things they hear and, finally, two more regulated breaths to end. The one we discussed at length in earlier chapters.

Again, we set the schedule of practice at twice a day during school and once at home. Again, we had very positive results in a very short time. There are no more instances of aggression and Tom is doing much better in school and at home. The principle reported to me in a recent IEP meeting how amazing it was when Tom had been coming out of the office where another student was sobbing and awaiting disciplinary action. Tom leaned down, patted him on the back and said, "Don't worry, it will be OK." It was a display the school staff had never seen before of pure compassion and perspective-taking. Tom is now a freshman, no longer experiences bullying because he has learned to self-advocate more, and is now tutoring other students having difficulty with math.

This progress was only possible because the professionals in that school took their roles as researchers and students seriously. They did not assume that their positions were solidified in an unchanging knowledge base. They came eagerly to the suggestions I offered and tweaked or added their own to strengthen the program for the student. This kind of collaborative effort between practicing therapists, parents, schools and students is a powerful combination and almost always results in positive progress. It requires that each member of the team bring openness and creative, outside-the-box thinking to the table with them. I have seen miracles worked when egos are left at the door, no one is assuming this is "another autism kid," and we look at the unique needs and strengths of the individual.

Meeting Safety Needs: Long-Term Effects of Social Exclusion and Bullying

I want to discuss the importance of bullying and social exclusion here, in the section on schools, because I think schools could do much more than they are about this situation and it has a profound effect on development. In the next section on socialization and social learning, we will discuss this at more length, but I would like to speak about what I have seen being done and what still needs to be done. Schools are certainly overstretched budget wise. Implementing new programs like an anti-bullying program requires effort, time and money. Most schools are drastically short on time and money.

Taking seriously the bullying that occurs is good. We want to do that. But when we take a zero tolerance, punishment stance towards the bullying we are, in many ways, simply continuing that culture. In my state (Missouri), bullying in schools was just made a felony offense. While that is certainly taking it seriously, I'm unconvinced it is the direction we should be going. Most bullies have been exposed to seriously less-than-ideal environments. They have often been bullied themselves at home or are the victims of neglect and/or abuse. Is the correct approach to take this child, who is responding to his environment, and punish him further? Certainly, we need to take it seriously, but I think the punitive approach is a response to damage control more than really thinking through what might be most effective.

What we truly need to be doing in schools is teaching compassion. In a freely available book called *The Heart of Learning and Teaching: compassion, resiliency and academic success*, Wolpow, Johnson, Hertel and Kincaid (2009) point out some fundamental truths about trauma, bullying and the success of teaching compassion and perspective-taking from a very early age in schools. Their first two principles of teaching compassion are "Always Empower, Never Disempower" and "Provided Unconditional Positive Regard" (p.72). The book goes further in laying out a well thought out and structured plan for teaching compassion in schools for both teachers (who are at risk of secondary trauma burnout) and students. The "Compassionate Schools Project" is another foundation dedicated to these principles and finding amazing results in the reduction of bullying. These methods have the added benefit of teaching compassion and perspective-taking to both those who would bully and those on the spectrum who may have difficulty in this area. In fact, when we look closely, we see that both the bullying behavior and the autism are rooted in trauma, and the perspective-taking parts of the brain are compromised in both instances.

Much of the problem is that schools can tend, like all our institutions, to become imbedded in bureaucracy and the belief that what has always worked, will always work. I simply question whether it has ever worked the way we are doing it, or if it is working as well as it could be and would like to challenge schools who have not implemented curricula around the teaching of compassion to do so. By implementing compassion curricula early, we create an environment where bullying is less likely to occur. In fact, the research indicates that teaching compassion, social and emotional skills results in both improved behavior and academic progress (Durlak, Weissberg, Dymnicki, Taylor, & Schellinger, 2011). I will cover the extreme effects of bullying in the chapter on social development.

Chapter 8: Social Development, Autism and Trauma

One of the major issues I run into with high-functioning young adults is difficulty with socialization that is nearly always rooted in social trauma. Bullying and social exclusion are repeated stories I hear from young adults who are struggling with finding their social place in the world. Often the bullying has been so intense that it leaves them with PTSD symptoms and completely changes the way they view and react in the world. On the rare occasion that I run into a young adult who was included socially in school, the difference in social functioning in adulthood is night and day. It is much more common that I run into a young adult in her 20's who is still greatly affected by the bullying and social exclusion she experienced even a decade earlier.

In homes where children must deal with alcoholic parents, the instability and unpredictable emotional outbursts and verbal violence literally begins reshaping the brain. I have heard from numerous clients the stories of lying in bed waiting for dad to come home and listening for how drunk he might be so that the child could decide if he needed to hide or protect his younger sibling from the onslaught. This constant need for vigilance changes the structure of the brain. It creates a constant, low level of anxiety and cortisol to be prepared for the inevitable. Because this system is unpredictable and unstable, the nervous system becomes attuned to an existence in a state of hypervigilance. This creates a heightening of sensitivity to perceived slight or potential harm.

Social trauma occurs when the repeated bullying and exclusion creates this same drip, drip, drip effect on the brain. The child does not know when or where the next rejection or attack will come from. In addition, the child already has a limbic region primed for a trauma response by autism. Remember our discussion of the over-connected brain and the enlarged amygdala. What almost any child would experience as a traumatic event is seriously intensified by the autism. The bullying and exclusion have very real and damaging consequences on social development.

When children hit middle school and junior high, they enter a development stage in life that Erik Erikson identified as "Identity Vs. Role Confusion" (Erikson, 1963). The major issue during this stage is the development of the individual's identity. Who am I? Where do I fit in with all this mess around me? It is a stage where the young adolescent begins to define where she fits in. The way young people do this is by looking to their peers for that identity. At this stage, our identity is very much found through reflection in the eyes of others. Good parenting can provide grounding and perspective if there are one or two instances of rejection. When mom and dad remind the young adolescent of who she is, and her friends see those good things in her, a mental equilibrium can be returned. If, however, the mental attack is consistent and the message of "you're weird" is repeated in the eyes of peers over and over, the effect of parents trying to counter that is likely to be minimal.

In my groups for high-functioning adults, we talk about that experience and how it leads to giving up on the idea of trying to fit in anywhere. If I were putting together a playhouse for my daughter and every time I made a mistake it shocked me, it would not take long for me to give up on that playhouse. Pain is a teacher, but when I am met with repeated emotional pain and there never seems to be an end to it, I simply stop trying. I never learn where I belong or what my purpose is in the social structure. Additionally, the brain becomes shaped in a way that even when someone does attempt to connect, it is met with suspicion as to motive simply as a matter of self-protection and preservation.

Erikson was clear that if the individual fails to complete one of the stages of development successfully, they will find it difficult, if not impossible, to complete the next stage. This is, in fact, what I see happening in my practice every day. The next stage according to Erikson is "Intimacy Vs. Isolation" and takes place from about 18-35 years of age (Erikson, 1963). It is this stage where people begin to risk intimate connection and build both intimate and sexual relationships. But if I am not convinced of my own worth or value, I will not risk further rejection. Not having an idea about identity keeps the individual from moving forward and risking further relationships and intimacy. It is simply easier to sit in my parent's basement and play video games than risk further hurt and rejection. I tell patients that I can guarantee them two things about relationships: First, they will be hurt. All people are broken and we break each other occasionally. Second, if they are paying attention to the lessons and growth opportunity provided, it will always be worth it. But getting them to buy in to that paradigm when they have a brain that is shaped to react with fear and anxiety at the very thought of connection is a monumental task.

I see this play out repeatedly in the groups that I lead in relationship development. Bullying is a core theme among members and became such a central theme that I began devoting two entire sessions to that discussion. Bullying became a recurrent theme throughout the group. Bullying with the neurotypical population can have very adverse effects, as we know from research, and can create increases in effects like depression, anxiety, isolation and even lead in extreme cases to suicide and self-harming. When we refer to the discussion of the ways in which the brain is primed for a trauma response in autism, we see that these results are seriously magnified. In addition to the heightened reactivity to trauma, there is another way I have noticed that the trauma affects the individual with autism. It is the ability to perseverate on the idea of "fairness" and to perseverate, in general, on the traumatic experience of bullying and social exclusion. Often, individuals on the spectrum will become hyper-focused on one subject. I have worked with many individuals who were hyper-focused in this way on Pokémon or Minecraft. I have noticed in my work that they can also become hyper-focused on the unfairness of life and on the emotional trauma created by that unfair treatment. This is in keeping with what we have previously learned about a brain primed to respond from the limbic region. Everything gets filtered through the "safe/not-safe" lens.

In many cases, the individual struggles to try and figure out "what is wrong" with them. They have been told so often that they are weird or broken that they have simply accepted that as fact. They begin to move through life thinking of themselves as "missing a piece" rather than just being different thinkers. In the process of trying to figure out what is broken, they internalize the bullying and every time they encounter difficulty in a social situation, that internalized bully reminds them of their own brokenness. Moving past this is extremely difficult, but entirely possible.

In one of my recent groups, we were watching the documentary *Autism In Love* (I highly recommend it) and when we had finished, I asked the group if, based on our discussion thus far in group, there were any observations that had particularly struck them. One of the members said that he felt the issues they were struggling with of vulnerability and intimacy were the same that everyone struggled with, but that the autism was magnifying the struggle a thousand times. I could not have said it more succinctly myself. The struggle with vulnerability and intimacy is not limited to autism. The big secret of humanity is that we are all broken. Autism simply magnifies the issue.

In my groups, we deal with this broken space in much the same way that we deal with sensory issues. We begin with mindfulness training. I hand out fidget cubes, fidget spinners and just fidgets in general in my groups (they are a HUGE hit) and we use them to begin simple grounding exercises in mindfulness. Next, we move on to learning emotional regulation and using the breathing and grounding techniques to slow down and release the limbic brain so that we can decide how we want to respond to the world around us rather than simply reacting to it.

Once we have slowed the emotional roll, we begin working on embracing vulnerability. I am very honest with them. I make no bones about the fact that if you enter the fray of intimacy and relationship, two things are a guarantee. First, you will be hurt. Relationships and intimacy mean being vulnerable and you will be hurt in the process. Second, it will be so worth it. If you are paying attention and learning the lessons life offers, even the hurt will be worth it. As human beings, we are wired for and function at our peak in connection with one another and the payoff is worth the pain. Convincing someone of this when she is uncertain of her own place or value is a challenge.

We begin the group and movement through social healing and growth by defining who we are in the world. We return to Erikson's "Identity Vs. Role Confusion" and begin by listing 10 things I am good at and 10 things good about me. Generally, discussion is opened with the difference and then participants have a week to complete the lists, at which time we share in the group the top three of each. The difference between the things I am good at and things good about me becomes the focus of the next session. Things I am good at are external while things that are good about me are internal.

We begin identifying talents and traits as a foundation to identity development. We begin the discussion of keeping the focus on the internal when deciding who we are and the ways that exclusion and bullying have forced our focus outward.

In the interest of honesty, we next look at three things we would like to improve about ourselves. This begins the discussion of inherent, but survivable, brokenness. Getting them in touch with the idea that it is OK to be broken is a new experience and begins rewiring the brain to be less reactive to mistakes. It is a part of every functional human being's growth process to look at the broken spaces and begin learning to heal them. Fundamentally, having the courage to face these spaces and grow out of them is the key to growth through trauma for all of us. Again, as my insightful group member on the spectrum pointed out, it is no different with autism…just magnified.

I often tell patients (both trauma patients and autism patients) that the broken spaces are what makes us beautiful. I compare this healing of broken spaces to the Japanese art of Kintsugi. In Kintsugi, the potter will make a vessel and then break it into pieces. She does this because then she can seam the broken pieces back together with gold, making it even more beautiful. You are Kintsugi, I tell them. If you focus on the broken places and pay attention to their healing, you can be even more beautiful than you had dreamed. On the other hand, living in our brokenness can leave us bitter, resentful and often ugly.

Knowing both my strengths and my weaknesses leads me to a stronger sense of self and identity and begins the process of identity formation for individuals. I tell them the power of knowing, in a deeply honest way, these things about myself is that no one can bully me any longer. If someone were to come to me and say, "Robert, you are one messy, unorganized dude!" I would smile, shrug and tell them I was working on it because I know that organization is not one of my strengths at times. It would not hurt my feelings and I would not run from that truth because I already have confronted and accepted that. If they were to approach me and say, "Robert, you're a horribly thoughtless and uncaring person!" I would think for a moment if I had done something to look that way and then would say to them, "You simply don't know me that well," because I know that is not true about me. I look for a moment at my behavior to insure I have not been misunderstood, but I know about myself that I am deeply caring and compassionate. These are my defined strengths and so I am unhurt by a misread or a hateful comment when it challenges that view.

Beginning the identity formation process allows us to move forward to risking intimacy. Erikson's stage of "Intimacy Vs. Isolation" can now be attacked successfully. If I have an identity that I can define, I can begin approaching others from a place of strength and confidence and know that I am worthy of connection out of those places. Resistance to social isolation and bullying is strengthened and the individual becomes more willing to take chances. Navigating the hurt becomes a matter of knowing oneself better and more deeply and because the individual has done the introspective work, there is a base of strength from which to do this.

It is a process for all of us, this risking, being hurt, healing and risking again. Many of the attachment disorders I see as a mental health therapist rise out of the undealt with broken spaces left by previous (generally very early) bonding relationships. Working through those past traumas, whether they are abuse at the hands of caregivers or bullying by peers, is often excruciatingly painful. Frequently with survivors of child abuse, I explain that this process of braving the world when attachment is both what you need and what you fear most will be difficult. I explain to them what my daughter taught me about butterflies. When the caterpillar crawls into the cocoon he liquefies. Except for a few neural cells that tell him what he will be, he becomes an amorphous goo. That must be a hellishly painful process. In fact, I am certain that if caterpillars knew what they were going to go through before earning their wings there would be far fewer butterflies in the world. This is a human experience. We are all broken. It is out of brokenness that we heal and grow. Autism magnifies the experience and makes the pain more difficult to navigate. But if the person has the courage and strength to stay with it, they learn to fly in spite of their differences. Their wings are amazing!

Chapter 9: Employment Issues

I will discuss some great programs for employment in this section as well as some of the struggles I have seen with parents trying to navigate seriously broken systems. But, for a fuller, better and far richer discussion of employment issues, you should read much of Temple Grandin's work in the area. This has been her focus for the past several years. I had the distinct pleasure of sharing a flight with her to Indianapolis for the Autism Society's national conference when we were both in Kansas City and she was going to be the key note speaker while I was simply presenting on the use of mindfulness in autism treatment. Her mind for data is what I remember most about that trip. She was an absolute wonk when it came to being able to talk about the specific validity and reliability of various research studies and I, being a fellow geek, loved it. I also remember the extensive discussion of thinking styles and how the tech industry was grabbing up kids on the spectrum. Her knowledge base in this area is huge. I was honored to have shared that brief few hours with her.

Temple Grandin has some excellent suggestions for teaching job skills to kids before they ever graduate from school. She breaks down how to approach jobs from a strengths perspective, considering how the brain of the individual processes and defines her employment history as a model in several of her works. In one instance, she refers to a student she knew who graduated college without having ever developed any job skills at all with some disdain at the lack of preparation he was given. Grandin is very good at pointing out natural proclivities of an individual and how that can and should be used in the employment approach. One thing I quickly discovered about Temple Grandin in our few hours chatting is that she is highly organized—a skill that I lack and very much admire in her. I have referenced a couple of her works on the web regarding employment in the works cited section, but really encourage the reader struggling with this issue to read her more extensive works on the topic (Grandin, n.d.), (Grandin, 1999).

I want to let parents and caregivers know that employment is a very real possibility for your child with autism. But you cannot count on schools to do the job in transitioning youth from graduation into employment. In fact, in my experience, schools and even vocational rehabilitation have done a poor job of doing this and the child is faced with full-time support that ends on graduation. In many cases, it feels as though the child hits adulthood and we suddenly decide she no longer has autism or need for support. Vocational rehab is overloaded, underfunded and understaffed. It is often a slow and frustrating process. But there is hope. Schools are getting better at this and there are programs that are wonderful out there if you know where to look. We will talk about a few of them here.

I want to start with Project SEARCH. When I was a case manager contracting through the state of Missouri, my friend, Beth Sherrill, got me involved with Project SEARCH just enough that I saw how amazing it was. Unfortunately, my involvement was minimal because I was working full time and finishing an internship and master's in counseling, so my time was short. However, I was able to research the program and discuss it with her extensively. The program is taking off in many states nationally and the statistics are amazing, to say the least. The goal of SEARCH is 100% employment for those who complete the program, and they are meeting that goal in the North Kansas City area.

Essentially the program enrolls the student for a fifth year of high school after graduation. This year of school is directed at three different three-month internships at a single job site. Here in the Kansas City area, Children's Mercy Hospital is one of the host sites that does an excellent job. The student shows up each day at the work site and there are generally employment meetings where the individual learns job skills, job prep and personal management skills needed for employment. Then she meets with the site supervisor and team to discuss how employment is going and spends the day focusing on training in an intern job position. Three jobs for three months over the school year. This gives the individual a real taste of the work world in addition to learning what his strengths, likes and dislikes are. There are criteria that must be met to be involved in the program, including extensive interviewing with the selection team and a promise of support from the parents in the program. It can be time intensive but is carefully laid out to insure success.

SEARCH is a model program in my view that should be seriously funded and expanded. I have repeatedly seen individuals who were offered full time, competitive wage jobs on completion. In fact, SEARCH has produced a book that I highly recommend in helping with the transition from school to work that is heavily based in the principles that work so successfully in their program. The book is called *High School Transition That Works: Lessons learned from Project SEARCH*. It is worth the forty-dollar investment and I have cited it in the back of this book as well.

Another program meant to help individuals with developmental disabilities prepare for life after high school can be found at an increasing number of universities by various names. At the University of Central MO, the program is called THRIVE. I had the pleasure of sharing a meal with one of the leaders of the program at the American Counseling Association of MO conference in 2014 and learned in depth about that program. For a deeper look than I can provide here, you can visit their site at https://www.ucmo.edu/thrive. There is a program at the University of MO Kansas City that is very much like this and it is known as PROPEL. Both programs are two-year college programs meant to provide individuals with skills necessary for transitioning into independent living and college attendance. In THRIVE, the individual lives on campus in integrated dorms with neurotypical peers. Having run into issues with these spaces before, I was very open about my concern with how the participants were received by their peers in the program. The program representative I was sharing a meal with assured me that they really were looked at as brothers and sisters who were kind of ushered in and almost protected in ways. There was, according to her, full acceptance in the program. I have since heard from program participants that this is indeed the case. The program provides training in life skills, provides group and individual counseling for adjustment issues and enrolls the individual in basic and manageable college courses with their neurotypical peers. It is essentially a slow start at adult, college life that allows the individual to decide what they would like to pursue in her future. This type of program seems to be catching on and I encourage parents to reach out to local universities through the education departments and see where they may exist.

Fundamentally, these programs share one approach: Start with the strengths. Start with what the individual does well and build on that. Know the style of thinking that the individual approaches problems with and begin finding work that fits into that paradigm. Temple Grandin talks about three major types of thinkers:

- **Visual Thinkers:** See the world in terms of photo-realistic pictures that race through their heads, but have difficulty with abstractions like algebra
- **Pattern Thinkers:** Good at math and music because they identify patterns easily. Developing story lines or following them in English class may be the difficulty here.
- **Word Fact Thinkers:** Individuals who put their talent for perseveration to use. They research

> and know every fact about certain topics. They
> would do incredibly well in libraries as book
> keepers, etc. (Grandin, n.d.)

This is only a small look at the types of unique thinking styles that individuals on the spectrum may express. The point here is that we should start with a look at the unique talents, abilities and even weaknesses of the individual and proceed from there. The aforementioned programs are very uniquely suited to doing just that. But, as Grandin points out in many of her books, anyone is capable of helping the individual with this type of introspection. Grandin was lucky that her mother was an educator who knew how to push her out of her comfort zone, even though I'm quite sure as a parent it hurt her at times to do so. This is a common issue with autism that we will discuss in the chapter I have titled *"To the Parents."*

Finally, I want to discuss one glaring and frustrating problem with the employment of even high-functioning individuals with autism. That is the problem of transportation. Especially transportation in moderately-sized cities with underdeveloped public options or more rural communities. Even in cases of very high-functioning individuals, transportation can become an issue.

Remember our previous discussion of executive functioning and the ability to make snap decisions one after another. This is exactly the skill needed to be able to drive oneself defensively and safely. This is exactly the reason that many individuals on the spectrum with very high IQ's have such anxiety that they simply cannot drive. Again, it is also something I see in cases of trauma when individuals become agoraphobic and anxious. The executive functioning has been affected by the history of trauma and the confusion that ensues feels unsafe and creates unacceptable levels of anxiety.

Some of these necessary driving skills can be repeatedly taught through practice and integration until they become a form of muscle memory, but not every person is able to handle the learning curve enough to overcome the anxiety and potential danger of driving. In these instances, I have repeatedly seen individuals who were perfectly capable of gainful employment but were living on disability income and trapped in poverty simply because there was no decent public transportation. I have seen young men get jobs in the competitive world only to lose them because they had no reliable way to get there. In my state, there is disability transportation that will take individuals to and from work for a minimal fee generally paid for by county tax boards. But even in this situation, if the individual lives in bordering counties, the transport will take him only to the county line and no further. Not a help. Counties, in my experience, have stubbornly refused to work together to figure out who is going to pay for what out of county tax funding and tax payers are unaware of the issue. In this instance, awareness becomes key and advocacy becomes the answer. We will discuss the power of advocacy in the next section.

Employment is a huge issue in the field of disability in general and it is fraught with controversy. Nothing is more important in the development of social skills and a sense of worthiness and identity than employment. I do not want to leave this chapter without impressing on the reader that if we work hard for 18 years to educate a person only to drop the ball when they are ready to jump into the world of adulthood, we have done nothing of value for them at all.

Chapter 10: Treatment Methods, Issues and Direction

Currently ABA (Applied Behavioral Analysis) is one of the premier treatment modalities for autism, especially in children. ABA is a very effective method in changing behavior and I would not want the reader to think that I am saying it is an inappropriate or ineffective treatment for autism. Certainly, the evidence, in many cases, is quite the opposite. My argument here is only that to begin with behavioral interventions without looking at what it is that is dysregulating the child is a bit like putting the cart before the horse. The argument that I often hear is that no matter the cause of the behavior, we can shape the behavior using ABA methods. This is often true. I simply feel we can do better than shaping behavior. If we make the child feel safe in the world the research indicates (as we will see) that the need for changing behavior is lessened and often removed.

We have seen previously how autism affects the child's brain in the same way that childhood trauma does. In fact, we have seen that the physiological changes in the brain due to autism are very much like the changes due to trauma. We find that the amygdala is often enlarged, the brain is over-wired and that the prefrontal cortex, corpus callosum and other significant areas of the brain are often times severely underdeveloped. Given this similarity it is, and has been, my argument that we must start by treating the autism as a trauma event and considering first the needs of the brain. Once we begin to treat the reactivity of the trauma-shaped brain, we can institute new learning through the application of ABA models. Maslow made it very clear in his work *A Theory of Human Motivation* that safety and security was the primary need of all humanity and unless that need is met, no new learning will take place (Maslow, 1943). This is why schools make sure to feed children breakfast and lunch when those might be the only meals they get that day. If they come to school hungry and thinking about meeting that basic need, no learning is going to take place. In fact, schools everywhere are seeing the benefits of accounting for ACEs (Adverse Childhood Experiences) in the child's life and the lack of learning that takes place if they are not accounted for. What I am saying here is that we must stop asking first how to make the child's behavior more acceptable and start looking at how we can make the child feel safe.

Until the child feels safe, they have no interest in learning new tricks. If I make them feel safe, they will follow me to the ends of the earth. Behavior is always communication. I see this with both trauma and autism. The communication is essentially this:

> *I am acting out because I want your attention and I want your attention, often, because I feel unsafe. Something is making me anxious, something has frightened me, something is confusing me and it's all leaving me without a clue how to manage and because I am little, and you are big, you are supposed to figure this out. Until you figure this out I will be banging my head on the*

floor, rocking uncontrollably, flapping my hands, yelling and spinning in circles or doing whatever else seems to work in the moment because this has simply become unbearable. I'm sorry if my behavior does not fit into your definition of "socially acceptable" but until you can help me find an alternative, this works for me.

Until we hear this message clearly and take steps to help the individual regulate internally, external behaviors will not change. Not for stars on a chart, special privileges, extra TV or computer time or any other external reward. Why would they? We must begin meeting these base safety and security needs first and then the behaviors will often take care of themselves. Indeed, when you make me feel safe and I no longer need my coping mechanisms, then I can clearly see the ways they have been failing me and change them.

The research points to this fact rather clearly and is the reason that I have lain out various models of treatment like sensory diets, sensory enrichment and mindfulness training. In fact, the research shows that when sensory needs are accounted for, the need for more expensive behavioral therapies drop off considerably, often to zero. In their study of sensory integration work with trauma survivors, Kaiser, Gillette and Spinazzola (2014) found that there was significant improvement in trauma survivors who were exposed to sensory integration treatment. In studies with children on the autism spectrum, the same has been found. In study after study, the findings support that sensory integration therapies reduce behavioral problems (Pfeiffer, Koenig, Kinnealey, Sheppard, & Henderson, 2011), (Schaaf, 2010) (Schaaf, et al., 2013). In some of these studies, behavioral issues were non-existent after treatment.

Again, when we begin making individuals feel safe, we reduce the behavior meant to cope with the feeling of danger. We reduce the reactivity of the amygdala and the mid-brain by teaching children how to control sensory overload. In several studies of sensory enrichment, it has been shown that there is even a thickening of the corpus and increased activity in the prefrontal cortex. On a flight to the Autism Society's national conference in 2014 in Indianapolis, I had the pleasure of speaking on the use of mindfulness in the treatment of autism. I had the even larger pleasure of meeting Temple Grandin at the airport in Kansas City, MO on the way there. We shared a flight and spoke at length about autism, horses and airline travel. She was a wealth of information and was the first to turn me on to much of the research about sensory enrichment and integration (her mind for statistics and detail is amazing). She told me about the research coming out and said she had even used the research to convince pork producers to enhance pig holding pens to reduce stress, increase weight and decrease bad enzyme production that resulted from stress so that the meat was better (Grandin, 1988). Indeed, the research she pointed me towards was showing a growth in regions of the brain and increased plasticity that were unknown only a few decades ago and led me to find article after article supporting the neural benefits of sensory enrichment since then (Aronoff, Hillyer, & Leon, 2016), (Hirase & Shinohara, 2014).

I have since implemented sensory diets, sensory enrichment and the mindfulness training previously discussed with client after client and found amazing results. Time after time I hear from parents, professionals and case managers that they have put forth months and years of behavioral therapies without significant progress only to find that when we change the direction of treatment and begin with meeting sensory needs, followed with mindfulness training, we find a significant reduction in behaviors. From there, the ABA therapies become much more effective when they are still needed.

It has become a significant goal of mine to begin changing the direction of treatment in a system that seems to be currently just throwing resources at parents hoping something works. I speak with parents all the time frustrated by increasingly trying supports that are not working because the direction of treatment has been paid little or no mind and services were simply placed in the home based on what "should" work. Jimmy, whom you will remember from chapter 6, was such a boy. His mother reported to me that she had just spent six months with an in-home ABA therapist and that he would spend the entire session biting, kicking and spitting. She held out little hope when I came in the home that we could help him. You could see in her eyes every time Jimmy approached me that she was just waiting for him to begin the assault. In addition to the mindfulness exercises that I worked with Jimmy on, we developed an entire sensory room in conjunction with his social services case worker. We ordered lights and a swing and a blow-up chair that could act as a squeeze machine and spinning toys. We put in place a diet that allowed him to come home from work and exist in this calming world for a time before the home activity started. Months later, Jimmy made a lot of progress and I felt that he would do better with another therapist who specialized in integrating movement with his therapy (interestingly, somatic therapy is foundational in healing trauma as indicated by such authors as Pat Ogden, Bessel van der Kolk and Peter Levine). His mother sent me an email some months later which left me in tears.

> *"Robert is the first provider to focus on my son's sensory needs as a primary treatment. Since we have implemented a sensory based therapeutic ideal, my son has made the most progress he has in years! He is no longer regressing, but PROgressing. And more*

importantly, I got my sweet good natured,
FUNNY kid back!"

This system works when we pay attention to the direction of therapies. We begin by assessing sensory needs and doing what we can to help the individual self-soothe and plan for self-soothing in a way that does not further separate them socially. Then we help them manage sensory issues and anxiety, OCD and other forms of dysregulation with mindfulness practices used on a daily basis and simpler, unobtrusive practices that can be used in the moment in a matter of seconds. This helps regulate the unregulated sensory issues that may still exist.

These same mindfulness practices can be used to teach emotional regulation in emotionally challenging or threatening situations. In high-functioning individuals, this often takes the form of social situations. Meeting new people involves risk and risk has often not paid off in the past. Navigating through mirror neurons and low vasopressin levels that leave one at a disadvantage for reading social cues, navigating through the emotional PTSD that prior bullying and bad social experiences have created, navigating through poor identity resolution and belief in self are all difficult in that split second of meeting someone new. If the individual has practiced slowing the breath and the body when these triggers arise, they are able to manage that anxiety much more effectively and move forward into uncharted and often frightening areas socially.

Finally, in children or those with cognitive impairment, if we are still seeing behavioral issues, we implement a well-designed plan meant to meet those behavioral needs. When we pay attention to what the child is really saying to us not just verbally, but with stemming and other behaviors and we pay attention to supports implemented in this manner and direction, the results are nothing less than astounding. I have case upon case and have read about many more where these methods have been successful.

Chapter 11: Final Notes to Parents

I want to divide this section up into several issues that I see recurring in my practice and over the past several decades of work in the field. I hope you will find some answers here that will help, but if you haven't found them all, then I want you to reach out to other parents, support groups, wherever you can. Just don't quit looking. I know you won't, because you've already survived this long through this hopefully not-too-dry book, looking for some of those answers.

Self-Care and Self-Regulation

I know, it's odd to see the first of this chapter start with self-care. But it's really the most important thing you can do for your child on several levels. I want to start here because I know how exhausting the search for help and services can be for parents. I have seen it in their eyes. I have watched as the emotion overwhelmed in my office and when I say "I think we can help this," the tears start to flow. Tears of hope and frustration and sometimes relief. I know how exhausting this can be. It is common for parents to simply be at their wit's end and that is why the care of the self becomes so very important. If you can learn to set aside time for your own care, you will be a better, more energized, more focused advocate for your kiddo the rest of the time.

We start with building your own mindfulness practice. It may sound silly, but it's incredibly important. When I was doing direct care and managing residential settings for individuals with developmental disabilities, I was often the go-to emergency guy. I was the guy they called at 1 AM when an individual was in inconsolable meltdown mode. Why? Because I was the guy that didn't get frazzled. I was the one who could control my own breathing and when someone is frightened and anxious and they look at you and you are not frightened and anxious they often begin to key in to that. Especially if they know ahead of time they can trust you. If a child looks at mom in the midst of anxiety and sees a relaxed, calm breathing, regulated energy, it feeds back to them the message that there is nothing to be afraid of. Mom is responding nonverbally with calm. She may be saying verbally, "Oh baby, I know, this sucks!" while she is responding with calm and compassion, but she is calm. Often, the child responds with self-calming in this moment. This is called attunement.

In my work with trauma survivors, once they have connected to me and we have come to a place where they trust me with the hard stuff, I find that I can often get them to change their breathing patterns and stay with me emotionally in the room simply by changing my own breathing. I no longer have to say, "Let's just take a deep breath." I simply do that myself and they will often respond in kind. That is attunement.

As an example, I had another therapist come to me at a seminar on mindfulness and emotional regulation and ask about how you would teach a toddler to regulate. I was told this child would become extremely anxious, begin shaking all over and then start holding his breath, which terrified the mother. Ultimately, the child won't be harmed and would, at worst, simply pass out and start breathing again. However, it was a terrifying experience for mother. I asked how she responded. The therapist recounted that generally mom was freaking out, picking up the child and begging it to breath or spraying water to startle it back to breathing. Laughingly, I asked how that was working. "Not so well."

The mother was simply confirming to the child that there was, indeed, reason to be afraid. The child responded by being even more anxious and terrified. What needed to happen was for mom to emotionally regulate, slow her own breathing and then pick the child up so that it could feel her heartbeat and breathing regulate as she soothed it. This tells the child that all is well. Mom is not afraid because there is nothing to be afraid of and you can calm yourself too whenever you are ready. On relating this to the therapist, she nodded her head and recounted that the child did much better regulating these episodes with father who was a very calm presence, but not always home.

So, when I am asked by a parent, "What can I do to regulate my child's meltdown mode?" my reaction is almost always, "Begin changing the way you respond." Practice your own self-care in the form of mindfulness and meditation to be able to handle those stressful moments better. Your child will begin responding to the calmer you, I promise.

Second, make sure you are making time for yourself and the other relationships that are important to you in the world. Spouses and other children often get lost in the mix when we are forced to focus on the needs of the needy child. It is important to try and find a way to make time for the others who demand less. Tending to those relationships will help you on several levels. First, they are an emotional stabilizer. If I am grounded to my spouse because we are spending quality time together, my ability to deal with insane and destabilizing events is much greater simply because I am grounded in the knowledge that this person has my back. If I am grounded with my "NT" children, then I am less concerned about their needs and they know I will be there when they have them, freeing me to focus entirely on the needs of the more demanding child when I have to and allowing them the security of trying to solve things on their own as they grow older.

Finally, carve out some time for self-dates. This may mean an hour-long hot tub, a massage, yoga class or simply some down time for leisure reading. Doing something that feeds you on a deep and calming level. As I type this, I can hear you now saying, "As if I could find that kind of time!" But I want to challenge you to find it because when you do, you will find you are paid back tenfold in time saved because you could not think clearly or quickly, or you were simply too exhausted to keep up. When you have learned to implement a way of being there for yourself on a regular basis you will find that you are more effective at implementing strategies for others. It really is that simple. Not easy, but simple.

Navigating Systems

One of the more difficult things about having a child with special needs is trying to navigate resources you are unfamiliar with and may not even know exist. In my state, a poor job is done of advertising the existence of state resources for autism. Often the states don't advertise the resource stream because they know it is severely underfunded and having everyone who needs it know about it would create overwhelming response and needs that could not be met at current funding levels. So, they make it exceptionally hard to get into and to navigate the system once you do manage to get in. Often parents are repeatedly asked to jump through hoops that are ridiculous and end up simply giving up. Not having the time to keep investing with no return, they often decide to simply go it alone even if they do know the system exists.

In addition, the system is designed to make it extremely hard and burdensome on providers of services. There is a reason that you will not find very many Medicaid providers in the states and that the states require Medicaid services be provided first. The providers are funded at about half of the rate they could make elsewhere, and the paperwork is overwhelming. I have literally seen providers in trouble because one of their caregivers put simply 1 – 4 as hours worked on the time sheet. Because he did not list AM or PM on the sheet, the oversight commission in my state was threating to take back thousands of dollars in funding. Speaking from a common-sense perspective, there is no reason anyone would be working with a child on social skills from 1 AM to 4 AM. These are the kinds of things that providers are asked to tolerate at pay rates that are laughable. So, there are six-month waiting lists for those dedicated few who agree to play within the system out of loyalty to the calling and need. With the system designed and run in this manner in many states, is it any wonder parents simply give up and go it alone?

My advice to parents then is not to give in to that system. Organize, stand on the tallest hill and scream at the top of your lungs until you can't anymore and then tag out and let the next person scream for you while you rest. I have repeatedly seen state government decide to slash and burn Medicaid services to families until families rose up and began screaming, became politically active and threatened the job security of legislators. Only then would the change happen and the pendulum swing.

Do not give up, do not listen to someone saying your child can't, or it can't be done for them. It is unproductive. I have seen dozens of children grown into non-functioning adults because the parents were told early, and believed, their child would never be capable. I have also seen parents who have pushed children to excel, pushed them gently beyond their comfort zones, and watched those children flourish to well beyond what anyone believed they were capable of. Do not listen to the nay sayers and lazy ninnies who cannot and therefore would rather not. They are limiting, they are wrong, and they are not what is best for your child. Keep pounding on doors until someone says they can and will help you.

I know I don't have to tell you that as a parent, but I also know it is bone tiring. Exhausting to the point that you no longer think straight yourself and feel bullied by the world. When things start to feel that way, you need to go back to the top of this chapter and read the part about self-care again.

Finally, understand that you will make mistakes. Little ones, big ones and ones in between, you will make them all. That's OK. As I tell my 16-year-old daughter, we only learn by screwing things up. Keep breathing. Keep determined. Keep engaged with both your kiddo and the system. Know that you may not be a rock star everywhere, but you are this child's rock star and they rely on you to help them navigate a confusing and trauma-inducing world. I have met very few parents who weren't well in touch with that already. I hope to meet more of you!

Appendix A: Sensory Assessment List

©Robert Cox, Life Recovery Consulting, 2016

Although I do recommend getting a good OT/PT to do this, I also understand that resources and time are often limited. So this sensory list and a few links to ways and means of setting up a sensory diet are a good start. If you can get the funding and find an opening with a good OT/PT, however, I think it is an invaluable resource for beginning.

Tactile Issues (Touch):

Issue	Seeks	Avoids	Neutral
Being touched specific areas (specify)			
Hugs, snuggling, etc.			
Clothing: tight, loose, materials (specify)			
Getting hands, face, etc., messy or wet			
Using towels after bath			
Crowds or personal space issues			
Walking barefoot			
Personal grooming (brushing hair, teeth, nails, etc.)			

Scores: _____ _____ _____

Proprioceptive Issues:

Issue	Seeks	Avoids	Neutral
Jumping, bouncing into things, climbing, hanging, etc.			
Perching in high places, risky bike riding, jumping from heights, other risky behavior			
Fine motor tasks (picking up small beads, etc.)			
Physically demanding tasks requiring muscle			
Having eyes closed or covered while walking			

Scores: _____ _____ _____

Vestibular Issues:

Issue	Seeks	Avoids	Neutral
Spinning in circles			
Shaking head from side to side or back and forth, hanging upside down			
Rocking			
Balance activities (biking, skating, etc.)			
Walking on soft deep carpet, snow, sand			
Riding in a car or on a sled, etc.			

Scores: _____ _____ _____

Vision Issues:

Issue	Seeks	Avoids	Neutral
Reading for longer than a couple of min.			
Shiny, spinning objects like pinwheels or chandeliers			
Hidden picture puzzles or mazes			
Going to crowded public places			
Light sensitivity or seeking			
Action packed, colorful TV or computer			
Using a kaleidoscope or looking through colored glasses			

Scores: _____ _____ _____

Auditory Issues:

Issue	Seeks	Avoids	Neutral
Loud noises in general			
Loud noises at specific frequencies			
Music, TV at too high or too low volume			
Conversation in noisy areas			
Concentration in noisy areas			
Rapid verbal instructions (games, etc.)			

Back and forth conversations			
Alone time			

Scores: _____ _____ _____

Taste and Smell Issues

Issue	Seeks	Avoids	Neutral
Certain food textures (specify)			
Strong citrusy flavors			
Spicy foods			
Tangy foods (Sharp cheese, etc.)			
Chemical smells (plastic, bleach, etc.)			
Crunchy foods			
Soft foods			
Perfumes, strong odors			

Scores: _____ _____ _____

Creating a Sensory Diet

Using the list above you can easily assess whether the individual is over or under sensitive in each region. Add the marks in each column. If there is an overwhelming tendency in one area or the other, then you need to start there first in developing the sensory diet. Below are some links to resources with lists of activities for meeting those needs. These activities will be hit and miss for the individual so it will require tracking what is and is not having an effect. Once you find a list of things that begin working, try and integrate more things like that.

Here is a link to a good article on Sensory diets and how to think about implementing them: https://www.sensorysmarts.com/sensory_diet_activities.html

This is a site that provides fantastic sensory activities for kids: http://www.kiwicrate.com/lists/sensory-play-activities/83

Essentially, you will need to be creative in putting the diet together and simply let the individual tell you (through behavior and verbally) what is working for them.

134

Works Cited

Aronoff, Eyal, et al. "Environmental Enrichment Therapy for

    Autism: Outcomes with Increased Access." *Neural*

    Plasticity, vol. 2016, 2016, pp. 1–23.,

    doi:10.1155/2016/2734915.

Ashburner, J., et al. "Sensory Processing and Classroom Emotional,

    Behavioral, and Educational Outcomes in Children With

    Autism Spectrum Disorder." *American Journal of*

    Occupational Therapy, vol. 62, no. 5, Jan. 2008, pp. 564–

    573., doi:10.5014/ajot.62.5.564.

Brand, Serge, et al. "Influence of Mindfulness Practice on Cortisol

    and Sleep in Long-Term and Short-Term Meditators."

    Neuropsychobiology, vol. 65, no. 3, 2012, pp. 109–118.,

    doi:10.1159/000330362.

Carney, Jolynn. "Perceptions of Bullying and Associated Trauma
    During Adolescence." *Professional School Counseling*,
    vol. 11, no. 3, 2008, pp. 179–188.,
    doi:10.5330/psc.n.2010-11.179.

Chang, Yi-Shin et al. "White Matter Microstructure Is Associated
    with Auditory and Tactile Processing in Children with and
    without Sensory Processing Disorder." *Front. Neuroanat.*
    Frontiers in Neuroanatomy, vol. 9, 2016,
    doi:10.3389/fnana.2015.00169.

Chen, Rong et al. "Structural MRI in Autism Spectrum Disorder."
    Pediatric Research, vol. 69, no. 5 Part 2, 2011,
    doi:10.1203/pdr.0b013e318212c2b3.

Corbett, Ba, and D Simon. "Adolescence, Stress and Cortisol in
    Autism Spectrum Disorders." *OA Autism*, vol. 1, no. 1,
    2013, doi:10.13172/2052-7810-1-1-348.

Courchesne, E., Pierce, K., Schumann, C. M., Redcay, E.,

Buckwalter, J. A., Kennedy, D. P., & Morgan, J. (2007).

Mapping early brain development in

autism. Neuron,56(2), 399-413.

doi:10.1016/j.neuron.2007.10.016

Daston, Maryellen, et al. *High school transition that works!: lessons*

learned from Project SEARCH. Baltimore, Paul H.

Brookes Publishing Co., 2012.

Daubenmier, Jennifer, et al. "It's not what you think, it's how you

relate to it: Dispositional mindfulness moderates the

relationship between psychological distress and the

cortisol awakening response." *Psychoneuroendocrinology*,

vol. 48, 2014, pp. 11–18.,

doi:10.1016/j.psyneuen.2014.05.012.

Digitale, Erin. "Low levels of hormone linked to social deficit in

autism." *News Center*, 22 July 2015,

med.stanford.edu/news/all-news/2015/07/low-levels-of-

hormone-linked-to-social-deficit-in-autism-study.html.

Accessed 8 Dec. 2016.

Durlak, Joseph A., et al. "The Impact of Enhancing Students' Social

and Emotional Learning: A Meta-Analysis of School-

Based Universal Interventions." *Child Development*, vol.

82, no. 1, 2011, pp. 405–432., doi:10.1111/j.1467-

8624.2010.01564.x.

Dölen, Gül, et al. "Social reward requires coordinated activity of

nucleus accumbens oxytocin and serotonin." *Nature*, vol.

501, no. 7466, Nov. 2013, pp. 179–184.,

doi:10.1038/nature12518.

Erikson, Erik H. *Childhood and Society. Second edition. Revised*

and enlarged. W.W. Norton & Co., New York, 1963.

Grandin, Temple. *Transition to Employment and Independent Living*

for Individuals with Autism and Aspergers.

www.grandin.com/inc/transition.employment.autism.asper

gers.html. Accessed 12 Nov. 2017.

Grandin, Temple. *Environmental Enrichment for Confinement Pigs*.

1988, www.grandin.com/references/LCIhand.html.

Accessed 26 Jan. 2018.

Grandin, Temple. *Temple Grandin: Choosing the Right Job*. Nov.

1999, www.autism.com/advocacy_grandin_job. Accessed

12 Nov. 2017.

Heinrichs, Markus, et al. "Oxytocin, vasopressin, and human social

behavior." *Frontiers in Neuroendocrinology*, vol. 30, no.

4, 2009, pp. 548–557., doi:10.1016/j.yfrne.2009.05.005.

Hirase, H., and Y. Shinohara. "Transformation of cortical and

hippocampal neural circuit by environmental enrichment."

Neuroscience, vol. 280, 2014, pp. 282–298.,

doi:10.1016/j.neuroscience.2014.09.031.

Howard, Sethanne, and Mark W. Howard. "Post Traumatic Stress
Disorder What Happens in the Brain?" *Washington
Academy of Sciences*, 2007, pp. 1–18.

Jain, Anjali, et al. "Autism Occurrence by MMR Vaccine Status
Among US Children With Older Siblings With and
Without Autism." *Jama*, vol. 313, no. 15, 2015, p. 1534.

Kaiser, Erika M., et al. "A Controlled Pilot-Outcome Study of
Sensory Integration (SI) in the Treatment of Complex
Adaptation to Traumatic Stress." *Journal of Aggression,
Maltreatment & Trauma*, vol. 19, no. 7, 2010, pp.
699–720., doi:10.1080/10926771.2010.515162.

Kim, Sang Hwan, et al. "PTSD Symptom Reduction With
Mindfulness-Based Stretching and Deep Breathing
Exercise: Randomized Controlled Clinical Trial of
Efficacy." *The Journal of Clinical Endocrinology &*

Metabolism, vol. 98, no. 7, 2013, pp. 2984–2992.,

doi:10.1210/jc.2012-3742.

Kirk, Virginia, et al. "Systematic Review of Mindfulness Induced

Neuroplasticity in Adults: Potential Areas of Interest for

the Maturing Adolescent Brain." *Journal of Childhood*

& Developmental Disorders, vol. 2, no. 1, ser. 8,

2016, pp. 1–9. *8*, doi:10.4172/2472-1786.100016.

Komiya, Migiwa, et al. "Lemon oil vapor causes an anti-Stress

effect via modulating the 5-HT and DA activities in

mice." *Behavioural Brain Research*, vol. 172, no. 2, 2006,

pp. 240–249., doi:10.1016/j.bbr.2006.05.006.

Lampen, Wendy. "See the world through her Asperger eyes."

YouTube, Ted X Delft, Dec. 2012,

www.youtube.com/watch?v=ZpNZJNQHAHw. Accessed

30 Nov. 2016.

Levine, Peter A., and Van der Kolk Bessel A. *Trauma and memory: brain and body in a search for the living past: a practical guide for understanding and working with traumatic memory*. North Atlantic Books, 2015.

Likens, Aaron. *Finding Kansas: living and decoding Asperger's syndrome*. New York, NY, Penguin, 2012.

Maslow, A. H. "A Theory of Human Motivation." *Psychological Review*, vol. 50, 1943, pp. 370–396., doi:10.1037/11305-004. Accessed 16 Jan. 2017.

Mccomb, Jacalyn J. Robert, et al. "A Pilot Study to Examine the Effects of a Mindfulness-Based Stress-Reduction and Relaxation Program on Levels of Stress Hormones, Physical Functioning, and Submaximal Exercise Responses." *The Journal of Alternative and Complementary Medicine*, vol. 10, no. 5, 2004, pp. 819–827., doi:10.1089/acm.2004.10.819.

142

Monks, Douglas A., et al. "Got milk? Oxytocin triggers

    hippocampal plasticity." *Nature Neuroscience*, vol. 6, no.

    4, 2003, pp. 327–328., doi:10.1038/nn0403-327.

Pfeiffer, B. A., et al. "Effectiveness of Sensory Integration

    Interventions in Children With Autism Spectrum

    Disorders: A Pilot Study." *American Journal of*

    Occupational Therapy, vol. 65, no. 1, Jan. 2011, pp. 76–

    85., doi:10.5014/ajot.2011.09205.

Schaaf, Roseann C. "Interventions That Address Sensory

    Dysfunction for Individuals with Autism Spectrum

    Disorders: Preliminary Evidence for the Superiority of

    Sensory Integration Compared to Other Sensory

    Approaches." *Evidence-Based Practices and Treatments*

    for Children with Autism, 2010, pp. 245–273.,

    doi:10.1007/978-1-4419-6975-0_9.

Schaaf, Roseann C., et al. "An Intervention for Sensory Difficulties

in Children with Autism: A Randomized Trial." *Journal*

of Autism and Developmental Disorders, Oct. 2013,

doi:10.1007/s10803-013-1983-8.

Schumann, Cynthia Mills et al. "Amygdala Enlargement in Toddlers

with Autism Related to Severity of Social and

Communication Impairments." *Biological Psychiatry*, vol.

66, no. 10, 2009, pp. 942–949.

doi:10.1016/j.biopsych.2009.07.007.

Schupp, Clayton W., et al. "Cortisol Responsivity Differences in

Children with Autism Spectrum Disorders During Free

and Cooperative Play." *Journal of Autism and*

Developmental Disorders, vol. 43, no. 10, 2013, pp.

2405–2417., doi:10.1007/s10803-013-1790-2.

Sofronoff, Kate, et al. "A Randomized Controlled Trial of a

Cognitive Behavioural Intervention for Anger

Management in Children Diagnosed with Asperger
Syndrome." *Journal of Autism and Developmental
Disorders*, vol. 37, no. 7, 2006, pp. 1203–1214.,
doi:10.1007/s10803-006-0262-3.

Spratt, Eve G. et al. "Enhanced Cortisol Response to Stress in
Children in Autism." *Journal of Autism and
Developmental Disorders*, vol. 42, no. 1, 2011, pp. 75–81.
doi:10.1007/s10803-011-1214-0.

Szalavitz, Maia, and Bruce Duncan Perry. *Born for love: why
empathy is essential-- and endangered.* New York,
William Morrow, 2010.

Tang, Guomei et al. "Loss of MTOR-Dependent Macroautophagy
Causes Autistic-like Synaptic Pruning Deficits." *Neuron*,
vol. 83, no. 5, 2014, pp. 1131–1143.
doi:10.1016/j.neuron.2014.07.040.

Teper, Rimma, and Michael Inzlicht. "Meditation, mindfulness and

    executive control: the importance of emotional acceptance

    and brain-Based performance monitoring." *Social*

    Cognitive and Affective Neuroscience, vol. 8, no. 1, 2012,

    pp. 85–92., doi:10.1093/scan/nss045.

Van der Kolk, Bessel. *The body keeps the score: brain, mind, and*

    body in the healing of trauma. New York, Viking, 2014.

Watanabe, Takamitsu, et al. "Mitigation of Sociocommunicational

    Deficits of Autism Through Oxytocin-Induced Recovery

    of Medial Prefrontal Activity." *JAMA Psychiatry*, vol. 71,

    no. 2, Jan. 2014, p. 166.,

    doi:10.1001/jamapsychiatry.2013.3181.

Wolpow, Ray, et al. *The heart of learning and teaching:*

    compassion, resiliency, and academic success. Olympia,

    WA, Office of Superintendent of Public Instruction

    (OSPI) Compassionate Schools, 2009.

Woo, Cynthia C., and Michael Leon. "Environmental enrichment as

    an effective treatment for autism: A randomized

    controlled trial." *Behavioral Neuroscience*, vol. 127, no. 4,

    2013, pp. 487–497., doi:10.1037/a0033010.

Yatawara, C J, et al. "The effect of oxytocin nasal spray on social

    interaction deficits observed in young children with

    autism: a randomized clinical crossover trial." *Molecular*

    Psychiatry, vol. 21, no. 9, 2015, pp. 1225–1231.,

    doi:10.1038/mp.2015.162.

Young, Simon. "Biologic effects of mindfulness meditation:

    growing insights into neurobiologic aspects of the

    prevention of depression." *Journal of Psychiatry &*

    Neuroscience, vol. 36, no. 2, Jan. 2011, pp. 75–77.,

    doi:10.1503/jpn.110010.

Zink, Caroline F., and Andreas Meyer-Lindenberg. "Human

    neuroimaging of oxytocin and vasopressin in social

cognition." *Hormones and Behavior*, vol. 61, no. 3, 2012,

pp. 400–409., doi:10.1016/j.yhbeh.2012.01.016.

Made in the USA
Middletown, DE
03 December 2022

16820479R00096